G000153663

The Devil's
DICTIONARY
of Economics
& Finance

Klaire Mun

Teach a man to fish and he will eat for life.
Give him someone else's fish and he will vote for you.

The Devil's
DICTIONARY
of Economics
& Finance

Pavel Kohout

Paul Kohout

19.3.2015

HPAP

Hyde Park Arts & Publishing, Ltd., London,
Great Britain 2014

THE DEVIL'S DICTIONARY OF ECONOMICS & FINANCE

Published by Hyde Park Arts & Publishing, Ltd., 2014

Copyright (c) Pavel Kohout, 2014
Illustrations (c) Klára Pernicová, 2014
All rights reserved.
Additional artwork: Dana Hejbalová 2014
Printed by AF BKK,s.r.o., Prague, www.afbkk.cz
For details on conditions of sale and bulk discounts please email:
devilsdictionary@hotmail.com

Hyde Park Arts & Publishing, Ltd.
25 Westbourne Terrace
W2 3UN London, Great Britain

http://www.hyde-park-publishing.co.uk
http://www.devilsdictionaries.com
Twitter: @DevilinFinance

Printed in Czech Republic
ISBN 978-0-9931226-0-6

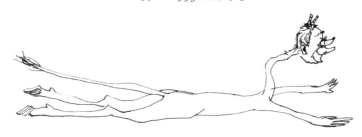

To the memory of Ambrose Bierce,

Ludwig von Mises,

and Murray Rothbard

CONTENTS

FOREWORD

Better the devil you know. Economics, however, is a largely mysterious and somewhat hellish subject for most people. There are many who love history, or the sciences—maths, physics, biology—but very few who love economics. This is not surprising given the alarming inability of economists to forecast anything, the numerous highly unbelievable—or just plain absurd—assumptions made by economic theories, and the ridiculous mumbo-jumbo that is used in order to obscure dodgy goings on or a lack of any real knowledge (or both). Normal people speak a normal language, don't they?

Yet despite all its deficiencies, the value of economics is indisputable. It may be a young, even immature science—like medicine before William Harvey's discovery of blood circulation in the 1600's—but it is still useful. If you don't believe this, just think of all those who have attempted to resist the economic way of thinking. The value of economics becomes only too clear when you consider the governments which have routinely ignored it; governments which have tried to cure their economic ailments by going back to the fiscal equivalent of bloodletting and leeches. Not to mention those more drastic remedies such as the decapitation of capitalists.

The world would be a better place if it were widely known that neither bloodletting nor 'out-of-thin-air' injections of money offer any real help. A well-known economist once remarked that it would be wonderful if economists could manage to get themselves thought of as humble, competent people on a level with, say, dentists. But it would be equally lovely if the basics of economics were at least as widely known as the benefits of dental hygiene.

Everyone should know the basics of finance, if only for financial reasons.

We can't all make billions from investments like Warren Buffett, the revered Sage of Omaha, who is right up there with Bill Gates in terms of personal wealth. Only the chosen few can be so spectacularly successful. Anyone, however, can avoid losing money stupidly, which countless people do without even realising it. Stopping losing money is a less spectacular feat than getting rich, but nonetheless extremely useful. As a financial advisor, I have enjoyed the most professional satisfaction when helping to thwart a financial disaster which a client would otherwise be headed towards.

Losing money in innumerable obscure ways is the reason why many people are poorer than they need to be, while some are much richer than they deserve. Interestingly, people too often eschew learning the basics of finance as they mistakenly believe it's a boring subject.

But this is by no means true. Finance can even have a certain entertainment value when served with a healthy dose of cynicism—which is exactly what this book is all about. You may be rich or you may be poor, but it is always best to tackle life's ups and downs with a touch of humour.

The author

THE DEVIL'S DICTIONARY OF ECONOMICS & FINANCE

ACADEMIC ECONOMISTS

1. The brightest and best of the intellectual leaders in the discipline.

2. PEOPLE who are clever enough to gain a clutch of academic DEGREES but rarely astute enough to get seriously rich; PEOPLE who teach about flexible LABOUR markets but crave tenured JOBS; scholars who develop elaborate theories about the BUSINESS CYCLE using sophisticated MATHEMATICAL MODELS but are unable to predict a RECESSION even when it is staring them in the face. See SOCIAL SCIENCES, INFERIORITY COMPLEX, MAINSTREAM ECONOMICS

Curious Fact: Fifteen thousand economists fail

James Galbraith, himself an ACADEMIC ECONOMIST, admitted that there were perhaps fifteen thousand PROFESSIONAL economists in the USA before the CRISIS of 2008, but that only a dozen or so of them could have predicted the CRISIS. Worse still, most of those predicted another kind of CRISIS that didn't happen. In fact, none of them were right; not one. A sorry state of affairs indeed.

Notable & Quotable

David Laibson of Harvard University said that *"There are very, very, very few economists who can be proud."* A NOBEL PRIZE winning economist, Robert Shiller, recently wrote: *"To a remarkable extent we have got into the current economic and financial CRISIS because of the wrong economic theory."*

Big respect to Galbraith, Laibson and Shiller for being honest about their profession.

> *"Modern academics must be able to keep writing and publishing even when they have nothing to say."*
> (Michael Billig, professor of SOCIAL SCIENCES, author of *Learn to Write Badly: How to Succeed in the* SOCIAL SCIENCES)

ACCOUNTING

Accounting has been called the "language of business". It all depends, however, on whether your accountant's command of the language is like that of Ernest Hemingway or the Brothers Grimm—or maybe Lewis Caroll.

ACCREDITED INVESTORS

1. Investors who are allowed to invest in higher RISK INVESTMENTS such as HEDGE FUNDS. The term generally includes wealthy individuals and organisations such as BANKS, INSURANCE companies, charities, CORPORATIONS, endowments, and pension funds, which are foolish enough to believe in the promised higher RETURNS, and wealthy enough to be able to withstand a substantial financial loss.

2. GREATER FOOLS

ACTIVE INVESTMENT STRATEGY
The optimistic belief that you can outfox the market. Don't try this at home.
See BUY-AND-HOLD, TRADERS

AMATEUR INVESTORS
Usually losers who have tried to experiment with ACTIVE INVESTMENT STRATEGIES at home. See CLIENTS

ANALYSTS
1. Financial PROFESSIONALS who immediately and correctly analyse all of the available information, thus making CAPITAL markets EFFICIENT. (Fictitious characters.)
2. Clueless and bizarrely overpaid DRONES. (Real characters.)
3. Highly skilled, well-paid, intelligent PEOPLE whose work is mostly futile; only the brightest of them are bright enough to realise this.

ASSET
1. A useful or valuable thing, person, ACCOUNTING item, or all of the above.
2. Something that was ridiculously overpriced when you bought it.
See BUBBLES, CAPM, GOLD DIGGER, MINSKY MOMENT

ASSET STRIPPING
Using legal loopholes to extract MONEY or PROPERTY from companies under management. See PRINCIPAL-AGENT PROBLEM, TUNNELLING

AUDITOR
An auditor is a PROFESSIONAL proofreader of the language of business, namely ACCOUNTING. He confirms that $2 + 2 = 4$ and makes sure that ASSETS are balanced with LIABILITIES. The auditor cannot, however, tell you if your business story will have a happy ending. Interestingly, the word auditor comes from the Latin 'audire', which means 'to hear'. Perhaps even auditors like hearing stories, but they are definitely not paid for doing it.

Since an audit is mandatory for most medium and large CORPORATIONS, auditors have always had plenty of work to do and always will. They are paid handsomely but rarely have time to spend the MONEY. As their time outside the office is very limited, they often date, marry and reproduce inside their profession. This may one day make it possible for a new species of human being to emerge.

BEAR MARKET
A period of broad and prolonged decline in the STOCK MARKET, during which PERMABEARS wake up and prognosticate the end of CAPITALISM as we know it and eternal damnation for STOCK MARKETS. Usually preceded by a strong BULL MARKET or BUBBLE. Usually followed by a strong BULL MARKET which most ANALYSTS fail to foresee.

BENCHMARK

A stock or BOND market index which defines AVERAGE RETURNS and which usually outperforms expensive INVESTMENT FUNDS and INVESTMENT MANAGERS. Why is this? It's the expenses. See BUY-AND-HOLD INVESTMENT STRATEGY

Curious Fact: Funds underperforming the index

The US STOCK MARKET index outperformed 66 per cent of American EQUITY funds between January 2004 and January 2014. More strangely, it was pretty much the same the previous decade. Most active INVESTMENT MANAGERS lagged far behind. So much for ACTIVE PORTFOLIO MANAGEMENT.

BETA COEFFICIENT
1. A random number believed to equal the systematic RISK of an INVESTMENT.
2. The reason why most BUSINESS PLANS are misconceived and most projects wrongly valued.
See CAPM

BILDERBERG GROUP
1. The world's de facto GOVERNMENT.
2. A closed club of ivory-tower intellectuals and POLITICIANS who are too distant from everyday life to understand anything truly important.

BILLIONAIRE
A person from the uppermost income group who is highly likely to have extraordinarily bad taste but unlimited means to pursue it. See MILLIONAIRE, OLIGARCHS, HARROD'S

BITCOIN
A virtual currency whose total volume in circulation is believed to be limited. (Unlike other virtual currencies such as the pound, dollar, EURO or yen, which may be multiplied by CENTRAL BANKS without restrictions or constraints.) The Bitcoin system is supposed to work in much the same way as the GOLD STANDARD, only with gold being replaced by faith.

The great advantage of the Bitcoin is the obscurity of its origins. You can complain about MONETARY POLICIES pursued by CENTRAL BANKS. You cannot, however, complain about the Bitcoin in the same way as you have no idea who is in charge of the system and who the Bitcoin's real originator was.

A more tangible advantage is that the Bitcoin cannot be created OUT OF THIN AIR. No CENTRAL BANKER can click his mouse and create Bitcoins at will.

Another advantage of the Bitcoin is that it is very young and has not been involved in any significant disruption or CRISIS, which have of course been caused by other CENTRAL BANKS many times in the past.

To date, no SECURITIES have been denominated in the Bitcoin. One possible explanation is a vast conspiracy against new competing CURRENCIES. Another reason may be the high VOLATILITY of the VALUE of the Bitcoin against "mainstream" CURRENCIES and the lack of clarity of its legal status in most countries.

BLACK MARKET
An illegal market which arises whenever and wherever GOVERNMENT regulations are divorced from reality to the point that the legal market cannot actually work.

BLACK-SCHOLES MODEL
A mathematical MODEL for option pricing (see DERIVATIVES). The MODEL itself is not that bad; it only seriously misprices certain option contracts. See DETAILS. Interestingly enough, most TRADERS keep using it even though they know it is not really correct: they use it because everybody else uses it.
See HERD BEHAVIOUR

BLOOD IN THE STREETS
A STOCK MARKET buying signal.

Curious Fact
Everybody knows the old saying about stocks, which are supposed to be best bought when blood is running in the streets. You may be under the impression that it was Baron Rothschild who said that. A little research RETURNS the following quotation:

Baron Rothschild (if his memory will bear one more legend) once advised the purchase of French Rentes.
"But," exclaimed he to whom the advice was imparted, "the streets of Paris are running with blood."
To which the Baron calmly replied: "If the streets of Paris were not running with blood you could not buy Rentes at this PRICE."
(Wall Street Journal, 10 May 1907)

Interestingly, the advice involved buying French GOVERNMENT BONDS rather than stocks. The PRICE of French GOVERNMENT BONDS fell to one half of their face VALUE during the violent times of the Paris Commune in 1871. The Commune's suppression was a brutal event which claimed around 21,000 lives, mostly on the side of the insurgents. A lot of blood indeed.

This all formed the background to the time when Baron Alphonse James de Rothschild (1827-1905) gave the above-mentioned advice to his CLIENT. Does this mean Rothschild was a brute beast making MONEY from his country's plight?

I think not. FRANCE was in an awkward situation in 1871. Baron Rothschild certainly helped his country by buying its GOVERNMENT BONDS. But more than that, he engineered France's economic recovery after losing the WAR to GERMANY. He was no dirty profiteer with blood on his hands.

BOND *(not James)*

1. The promise that the borrower will repay his DEBT to the lender, at a certain date, to the full amount, together with the coupon interest, in a properly debased and perhaps completely worthless CURRENCY.

2. SECURITIES which usually YIELD such a meagre return that no sane INVESTOR would buy them for himself or herself; usually purchased, therefore, on behalf of unsuspecting CLIENTS.

3. An INVESTMENT which is most prone to the RISK of INFLATION.

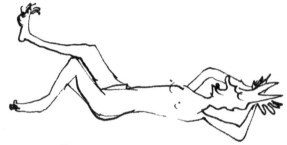

BOOM

An era of PROSPERITY usually caused by CREDIT EXPANSION and regularly followed by 'bust' (RECESSION), and sometimes by a CRISIS and a CREDIT CRUNCH.

BOSS

1. The person to whom you must report. Usually a hopelessly ancient grey-haired dim-witted fossil with a preposterously high salary and a fully paid-off MORTGAGE on his six-bedroom mansion. See LEADER

2. Verb: to boss somebody—to give somebody orders in a domineering manner, to harass somebody.

Notable & Quotable
"The man who gives me employment, which I must have or suffer, that man is my master, let me call him what I will." (Henry George)

BRIC

The famous (or perhaps infamous) acronym denoting four EMERGING MARKETS: BRAZIL, RUSSIA, INDIA, and CHINA. Coined in 2001 by Jim O'Neill, then a Goldman Sachs ANALYST. BRIC EQUITY PRICES indeed surged 6.6 times at the peak of the HYPE within six years of the publication of O'Neill's paper. The BUBBLE has been deflating for more than six years since, thereby causing much disappointment among naïve AMATEUR INVESTORS. See INVESTMENT HORIZON

BUBBLES

1. Speculative bubbles occur when the PRICE of ASSETS (EQUITIES, PROPERTY, COMMODITIES) shoots up well beyond reasonable levels. PRICE bubbles appear when the majority of INVESTORS rely on the theory of a GREATER FOOL or the EFFICIENT MARKET HYPOTHESIS.

2. Credit bubbles, which cause BOOMS, materialise when a CENTRAL BANK leaves INTEREST RATES too low for too long a time in order to mitigate a RECESSION or the stagnation of ECONOMIC GROWTH. A credit bubble is usually followed by a CREDIT CRUNCH.

See DOT.COM MANIA, TULIP MANIA

BULL MARKET

A period of persistent growth in STOCK MARKETS. When it lasts too long, stock PRICES may soar, at which point most AMATEUR INVESTORS buy EQUITIES in large volumes. Shortly after these PEOPLE have invested their life's SAVINGS, BUBBLES burst. See Eugene FAMA

BUREAUCRACY

A system of GOVERNMENT in which most of the important decisions are taken by STATE officials rather than elected representatives (Oxford English Dictionary).

Notable & Quotable

"A BUREAUCRACY is designed to maximize the distance between a decision-maker and the RISKS of the decision." (Nassim Nicholas Taleb)

"Rational BUREAUCRATS will always and everywhere seek to increase their budgets, thereby contributing strongly to STATE growth." (William Niskanen)

"An official wants to multiply subordinates, not rivals; officials make work for each other." (Cyril Northcote PARKINSON's laws on BUREAUCRACY)

See MORAL HAZARD, OTHER PEOPLE'S MONEY, OLIGARCHY

BUREAUCRAT
An official who is paid with OTHER PEOPLE'S MONEY. He or she therefore believes that those other PEOPLE are their subjects. Often recruited from losers who failed to find a JOB in private business. See PUBLIC SERVANT

Notable & Quotable
"The multiplication of careers opened by a developing BUREAUCRACY *tempts members of the classes regulated by it to favour its extension, as adding the chances of safe and respectable places for their relatives."*
(Herbert Spencer: *The Man Versus the* STATE, **1892**)

BUSINESS CYCLE
An irregular, perfectly acyclic and unpredictable series of ups and downs in GDP. The term "cycle" is used because it is conveniently short, simple and misleading. Fluctuations in GDP growth—BOOM, RECESSION, trough, recovery, further BOOM—are caused by INVESTMENTS and MALINVESTMENTS, mostly in construction and PROPERTY. See RECESSION, FORECASTING

BUSINESS PLAN
A complex projection of future sales, costs and profits, which never really happens the way it has been planned.

BUSINESS SCHOOL
An expensive school where they teach you how to make BUSINESS PLANS.

BUY-AND-HOLD INVESTMENT STRATEGY

1. A passive approach to investing which eschews the frequent buying and selling of securities and assumes that trading costs outweigh the benefits of market timing. Buy-and-hold therefore usually beats ACTIVE INVESTMENT STRATEGIES.

2. An excuse used by INVESTMENT BANKERS and ANALYSTS to explain to their CLIENTS why the VALUE of purchased SECURITIES keeps falling during BEAR MARKETS: *"Well, I know it's not a good time now, but hold on. It's a long-term INVESTMENT strategy, and you'll be better off buying-and-holding rather than selling in a panic."* Oddly enough, this advice usually works better than selling in a panic!

See INVESTMENT DECISION CYCLE

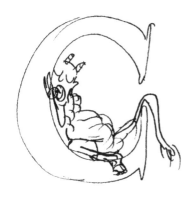

CANCER

A serious life-threatening illness which becomes less pressing in times of serious financial CRISIS. As the Greek minister of health said: *"Illnesses like cancer are not considered urgent, unless you are in the final stages."* See GREECE

CAPITAL

1. A large amount of MONEY you will never have.
2. Anything that can be used to produce WEALTH.
3. The main part of the title of an influential book by Karl MARX, which supported the mass destruction of CAPITAL in countries which are now called EMERGING MARKETS, particularly RUSSIA and CHINA. See LABOUR

CAPITALISM

1. A fictitious in-theory-only system in which PEOPLE's economic relations are based on the grounds of voluntary exchange; the GOVERNMENT acts merely as the guarantor of law and order.
2. The reason for everything bad and rotten in the world.
3. An economic system in which you can buy whatever you need or want as long as you have enough MONEY to pay for it.
See CAPITAL, SOCIALISM, COMMUNISM

Curious Fact: SOCIALISM *older than* CAPITALISM
The word "SOCIALISM" has been in use much longer than CAPITALISM, even though the idea of SOCIALISM is historically much more recent. This is because PEOPLE (especially CAPITALISTS themselves) considered CAPITALISM as the norm and never needed a special word for it. Since the early 20th century, "CAPITALISM" as a term for describing a market economy has been used mainly by its critics.

Notable & Quotable
Question: What is the difference between SOCIALISM and CAPITALISM?
Answer: CAPITALISM makes social mistakes while SOCIALISM makes CAPITAL mistakes. (Michael E. Adams, @M_E_Adams)

CAPITALIST
A person who uses their WEALTH to invest in trade and industry for profit in accordance with your needs and DESIRES. (What an insidious way of making MONEY, isn't it?)

CAPM OR CAPITAL ASSET PRICING MODEL
The misjudged notion that higher RETURNS on EQUITIES compensate for the higher RISK. Like many other strange ideas rewarded with the pseudo NOBEL PRIZE. See BETA COEFFICIENT

Curious Fact: STOCK MARKET *and* HYPERINFLATION
ACADEMICS are wrong to think that EQUITY RETURNS compensate for RISK. In fact, it is primarily INFLATION which drives up the PRICE of EQUITIES, PROPERTY and COMMODITIES. The PRICE of these ASSET classes does not increase as a reward for RISK but because of INFLATION.

A salient example. The EQUITY index MSCI BRAZIL appreciated an incredible 239,545,768.6 times from December 1987 to December 1994 in local CURRENCY. This was due only to HYPERINFLATION, which provided a total dollar return of a very enjoyable 634.5 per cent over the seven years. Did this represent a reward for higher EQUITY RISK? Not at all. Brazilian BONDS were, in fact, the risky INVESTMENT. The holders of BONDS in local CURRENCY got completely wiped out. See INFLATION, HYPERINFLATION

CENTRAL BANK
A GOVERNMENT-granted monopoly BANK that is authorised to print MONEY. Only MONEY counterfeited by a CENTRAL BANK is legal. See MONEY (fiat), OUT OF THIN AIR, INFLATION

CENTRAL BANKER

A highly skilled financial PROFESSIONAL—usually possessing enviable ACADEMIC credentials—who knows only two tools: cutting INTEREST RATES and producing fiat MONEY OUT OF THIN AIR.

CFA (CHARTERED FINANCIAL ANALYST)

A person who has been certified as unnecessarily clever to work in finance.

CITY OF LONDON, *The*

A LONDON borough which rules GREAT BRITAIN and possibly the world. One of the preferred targets of Nazi bombers during the Battle of Britain, and EU TAX commissioners during these modern times of enduring peace and friendship in EUROPE.

CLASSICAL LIBERALISM

A theory of the MARKET ECONOMY based upon the naïve idea that the STATE can be kept in reasonable proportion to the size of the economy. Despite being so obviously crude and unsophisticated, classical liberalism allowed Western countries to prosper and prevail over the rest of the world during the 18th and 19th centuries. See LAISSEZ-FAIRE, LIBERALS

CLIENTS *(of investment funds, managers)*

1. Happy PEOPLE who have something to be managed.
2. PEOPLE whose own mistakes may be much costlier than those committed by INVESTMENT MANAGERS.
See AMATEUR INVESTORS

COLONIALISM

A process during which a more viable and aggressive civilisation captures lands originally inhabited by natives. See LONDON, FRANCE

COMMODITIES

Materials such as oil, gold, orange juice and pork bellies, which are traded in exchanges. A ground for SPECULATION and a quick and easy way to lose your CAPITAL.

COMMON GOOD

A noble vision that has tempted many to try to create a new and better world but always end up destroying the old one. See SOCIALISM, COMMUNISM, DICTATORSHIP

Notable & Quotable

"Gemeinnutz geht vor Eigennutz" ("The COMMON GOOD before the private good"). (Motto from the book *Der nationale Sozialismus* by Rudolf Jung, 1922. This became Hitler's basic stance on the subordination of the economy to the national interest.)

"Social inequalities are acceptable only if they are in the interest of all." (Thomas Piketty, CAPITAL in the 21st Century, 2014. Here we go again.)

"A SOCIETY that puts equality—in the sense of equality of outcome—ahead of FREEDOM will end up with neither equality nor FREEDOM." (Milton FRIEDMAN, *Free to Choose*, 1980)

COMMUNISM

1. The opposite of CAPITALISM. *"Under CAPITALISM, man exploits man. Under COMMUNISM, it's just the opposite."* (John Kenneth Galbraith, quoting what he described as an old Polish joke)

2. An ECONOMIC system in which you can usually buy whatever you need or want as long as you have hard CURRENCY, good connections and access to the BLACK MARKET.

3. A modern surrogate of religion, shamefully proven false by a series of experiments in RUSSIA, CHINA, Cambodia and a number of other countries. See CAPITALISM

Notable & Quotable

"To each according to his needs; from each according to his ability." (Karl MARX. Believe it or not, this is the definition of COMMUNISM which school children in communist countries were taught. Of course, even the children knew it was ridiculous.) See SOCIETY, REAL SOCIALISM

"COMMUNISM is great in theory, it has just never been implemented properly." (A persistent argument of leftists who never really experienced COMMUNISM; in fact, it's exactly the other way round: COMMUNISM is utterly wrong in theory but has been implemented perfectly.)

COMPETITION
1. The most efficient mechanism ever devised for the unleashing of human energy.
2. The rat race. An endless, self-defeating and pointless pursuit.
See CAPITALISM, SOCIALIST STATE

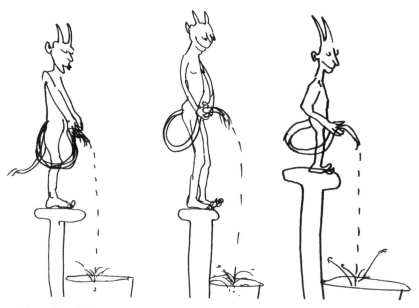

Notable & Quotable
"COMPETITION is merely the absence of oppression." (Frédéric Bastiat)

Curious Fact: COMPETITION in the Soviet Union
In the history of mankind there has hardly been any more strict command-and-control-based economy than the Soviet Union. Soviet LEADERS loathed CAPITALISM and everything related to it. They abhorred COMPETITION more than anything else because it was associated with FREEDOM, choice, individualism, creativity and independence—everything that has ever been the very antithesis of COMMUNISM.

Yet in the most strategic industry Soviet POWER depended upon, even the communists must have accepted COMPETITION. In a STATE with only one BANK and with a system which rationed almost everything, there were as many as fifty competing aerospace design bureaux covering all branches of the aerospace industry. Mikoyan-Guryevich, Tupolev, Sukhoi and others worked simultaneously on different projects, much the same way as Boeing, Lockheed, Grumman and Rockwell.

There was, of course, a difference. None of the founders of those design bureaux owned a share in them, at least until the fall of the USSR. COMPETITION was considered a necessary evil and tolerated as such. Private PROPERTY, however, was never tolerated in the Soviet Union. The consequent lack of motivation and the ubiquitous mismanagement in all spheres of the economy was the primary cause of the Soviet economic debacle.

COMPETITIVENESS
1. The ability to compete in the INTERNATIONAL TRADE of goods, CAPITAL and ideas; the existence of COMPETITION.
2. A poor excuse for cutting wages and salaries.

CONFISCATION, CONFISCATORY RATES OF TAXATION
Many countries experimented with extremely high rates of TAXATION hoping that TAX revenues would increase in proportion to TAX rates. Surprisingly (or perhaps not so surprisingly), a 95 per cent marginal income TAX rate applied in GREAT BRITAIN during wartime and, even deep into the post-WAR period, resulted in dismal ECONOMIC GROWTH and not quite so impressive TAX revenues.
See PROGRESSIVE TAXATION

Curious Fact: High TAXATION *in* INDIA
In the early 1970's, there was a combined income TAX rate of up to 97.75 per cent in INDIA. Was it auspicious for the country's PROSPERITY? Not really.

CONSERVATIVE
1. Someone who is against REVOLUTIONS and other sudden changes, claiming that the current rulers are already bad enough.
2. A political movement which keeps TAX RATES and PUBLIC EXPENDITURE levels high when it replaces SOCIALISTS in POWER, so as to conserve the WELFARE STATE.
See RADICAL

CONSTITUTION

A legislative instrument which proclaims certain basic rules and RIGHTS, such as the RIGHT of the GOVERNMENT to collect TAXES, spend beyond its means, and place the burden of DEBT on future generations.

CONSUMER PRICE INDEX (CPI)

The official measure of INFLATION. It is based upon the price of a basket of goods and services purchased by households for their own CONSUMPTION (not for resale). This means that the PRICE of a cremation is included in the CPI (because funeral services undoubtedly represent household final CONSUMPTION), but the PRICE of PROPERTY is not (because your home is classified as an INVESTMENT, and therefore not included in the CPI). A PROPERTY BUBBLE can therefore occur without the CPI moving very much at all.

Curious Fact: BOOM *in grave* PRICES

According to the Bloomberg news agency, the PROPERTY BOOM has increased costs well into the afterlife. *"At the end of the day, it's like any other piece of real estate,"* says Amy Cunningham, a New York STATE licensed funeral director. *"*PRICES *have conspired to put burials out of the range of most* PEOPLE*'s budgets."*

Every week, about 1,000 New Yorkers die. Manhattan is running out of room for them. Further out in Brooklyn, PRICES of plots for the deceased and apartments for the living are at record highs. A 756 square-foot mausoleum site in Green-Wood Cemetery, nestled on the edge of Brooklyn's Park Slope neighbourhood, costs $320,000. A 1,800-square-foot single family home across the street sold for $245,000 in 2009. Today it's worth $1 million, according to the website Zillow Inc.

No BUBBLE in the PRICE of a cremation has been observed; however, in Asian megacities, even space for urns is in short supply.

CONSUMPTION

1. The meaning of life.
2. A major component of GDP.
3. The secret object of DESIRE of most poor RADICALS and DEGROWTH activists.
See MONEY, RADICAL, SEX, ZERO GROWTH

CONVERGENCE

1. The notion that poorer countries or regions should catch up with DEVELOPED economies.
2. The observed fact that poorer countries or regions are indeed able to catch up with DEVELOPED economies, especially when it comes to the burden of DEBT and PROPERTY PRICES.
See SUBSIDIES, DEVELOPING COUNTRIES, EMERGING MARKETS

CORPORATION

1. Yet another root of all evil in the world.
2. Something you hate to work for but mustn't leave; a voluntary form of slavery.
3. Organisations which produce everything you ever needed for your life, like Big Macs, MacBooks and McJobs.

Notable & Quotable
"We need to get CORPORATIONS *out of* POLITICS. *"*
(The New York Times Company. A CORPORATION with sales exceeding $1.5 billion and market capitalisation of over $2 billion.)

CORRUPTION

Definition differs according to whether you are offering the bribes, receiving the bribes, or are the hapless TAXPAYER who is going to pay for its consequences:
1. A lubricant for business.
2. An additional tax burden, the proceeds of which end up in private pockets rather than the GOVERNMENT treasury.
3. An ECONOMIC system in which you can buy whatever and whomever you need or want as long as you have MONEY and connections.
See SYSTEMIC CORRUPTION, SUBSIDIES

COPYRIGHT

A concept you will probably consider utterly useless until you create something valuable. See INTELLECTUAL PROPERTY

Curious Question: Is COPYRIGHT *good for creativity?*
Does copyright protection stifle creativity or support innovation? As long as you remain a consumer, you probably hate paying for something you can download for free. When you create something valuable, your view of COPYRIGHT changes in the blink of an eye.

CREDIT
DEBT viewed from the other side.

CREDIT CARD
A sophisticated way of convincing poor PEOPLE to stay poor and become burdened with DEBT on top of their POVERTY. See GDP

Notable & Quotable
"CREDIT is what enables PEOPLE *to spend* MONEY *they haven't earned to buy things they don't need in order to impress* PEOPLE *they don't like."*
(Vikrant Parsai)

Curious Fact: MONEY *matters in* LOVE
In a study commissioned by Creditcard.com, about **70** per cent of women said they would break off a relationship if they found their partner had lied about their ability to pay routine bills. That's the same percentage of women who would stop seeing someone with a criminal record. Two out of three women consider secret CREDIT CARD DEBT a relationship deal-breaker, and **55** per cent would break it off if they found their partner was heavily in DEBT.

Men are more tolerant. Just over 50 per cent would terminate a relationship over lying about bill paying or secret CREDIT CARD DEBT, and just 37 per cent say heavy DEBT is reason enough to call it all off.

Participants in the study were also asked to evaluate the statement: "If you were about to get seriously involved with someone, you would want to know your partner's CREDIT score." About 57 per cent of women and 47 per cent of men agreed strongly or fairly strongly with that sentiment.

The strongest evidence of LOVE is sacrifice, or so the saying goes. Although somewhat more prosaic, it also involves MONEY.

CREDIT CRUNCH

When BANKS are afraid to grant new loans or extend old ones as their RISK managers believe that CREDIT quality may go bad. A CRISIS of LIQUIDITY therefore occurs: businesses don't have enough MONEY so they cut INVESTMENTS and reduce the workforce. As a result, an economic RECESSION or CRISIS starts and CREDIT quality does indeed go bad. A CREDIT CRUNCH is usually associated with a BANKING CRISIS. See BAILOUT, BUSINESS CYCLE, CRISIS, ALAN GREENSPAN

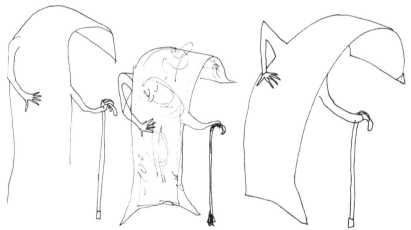

Curious Fact: CREDIT CRUNCH *was the ultimate cause of WWII*
Between 1929 and 1933, as many as 4,000 US BANKS (out of 12,000) went bust, causing a CREDIT CRUNCH and the GREAT DEPRESSION. At the same time, in GERMANY, BANK defaults caused a major CREDIT CRUNCH, which in turn led to mass UNEMPLOYMENT. In January 1933, political POWER was seized by you-know-who. A CREDIT CRUNCH was therefore the ultimate cause of WORLD WAR II.

CREDIT EXPANSION
A period of growth in terms of credit and GDP, usually fuelled by an EXPANSIVE MONETARY POLICY.

Notable & Quotable

"*The popularity of* INFLATION *and* CREDIT EXPANSION, *the ultimate source of the repeated attempts to render* PEOPLE *prosperous by* CREDIT EXPANSION, *and thus the cause of the cyclical fluctuations of business, manifests itself clearly in the customary terminology. The* BOOM *is called good business,* PROSPERITY, *and upswing.*

Its unavoidable aftermath, the readjustment of conditions to the real data of the market, is called CRISIS, *slump, bad business, depression.* PEOPLE *rebel against the insight that the disturbing element is to be seen in the* MALINVESTMENT *and the overconsumption of the* BOOM *period and that such an artificially induced* BOOM *is doomed. They are looking for the philosopher's stone to make it last.*"
(Ludwig von MISES, **1940**)

CRISIS
Crises may come in different shapes and sizes. Choose your favourite:
- Banking crisis: Too many loans in the good times make too many bad loans in the bad times. Think Ireland, SPAIN. See CREDIT CRUNCH
- Currency crisis: Occurs when the CENTRAL BANK maintains the CURRENCY exchange rate a long way from the EQUILIBRIUM (usually an overvalued CURRENCY).
- Budget crisis: The GOVERNMENT has too much DEBT and nobody is willing to lend it more MONEY or buy more BONDS. Think GREECE.
- Economic crisis: An unusually deep and prolonged RECESSION.
- Financial crisis: A generic name used by POLITICIANS and journalists who are unable to distinguish between particular types of crisis.

Notable & Quotable

"RECESSION *is when your neighbor loses his job. Depression is when you lose yours. And recovery is when Jimmy Carter loses his.*" (Ronald Reagan)
"*He who smiles in a* CRISIS *has found someone to blame.*"
(Michelle Beeler, @Michelle_OKC)

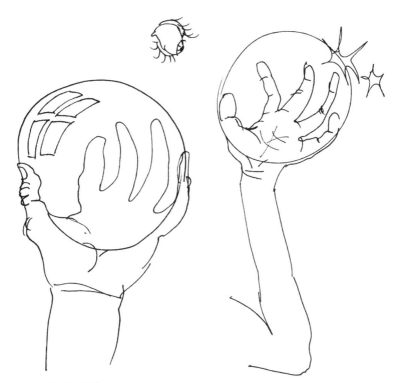

CRYSTAL BALL
A reliable FORECASTING device. In rare moments of frankness, ANALYSTS admit to not being in possession of one.

CURRENCY
A universal medium of exchange and VALUE storage which keeps losing its VALUE year by year due to the EXPANSIVE MONETARY POLICY of CENTRAL BANKS.
See FORGERY, QUANTITATIVE EASING

CURRENCY DEBASEMENT
1. Small scale: a serious crime, also known as FORGERY.
2. Large scale: a CENTRAL BANK policy, also known as EXPANSIVE MONETARY POLICY or DEVALUATION.
See DEPRECIATION, QUANTITATIVE EASING

CURRENCY UNION

The organisation of two or more countries sharing one CURRENCY, usually accompanied by the firm belief that they are worse off for that very reason.

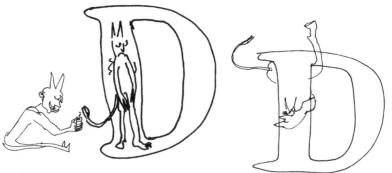

DATA MINING

1. In the good old pre-CRISIS days of the 1990's, data mining used to be considered a grave sin against proper statistical analysis. Data mining was a disrespectful label attached to the hectic search for hidden relations in data, which may often have led to SPURIOUS CORRELATIONS and therefore have been considered unscientific.

2. The main method of producing scientific papers practised by ACADEMIC ECONOMISTS today.

DEATH
Yet one more taxable event in the human life.

DEBT
1. A financial obligation with side effects. If I owe you £100, I have a problem. If I owe you £1,000,000, you have a problem.
2. An instrument of POWER: if a country is sufficiently indebted, it loses its SOVEREIGNTY and is subjugated to lenders.
See CREDIT, PUBLIC DEBT, SUBSIDIES

Notable & Quotable
"I like my players to be married and in DEBT. *That's the way you motivate them."* (Ernest "Ernie" Banks, a famous baseball player and coach)

DEBTOR
Somebody who owes MONEY. The Oxford Thesaurus of English offers the following synonyms: borrower, mortgagor; bankrupt, bankrupt person, insolvent, defaulter. Just so that you know where you are heading when take on a MORTGAGE or pay with a CREDIT CARD. See BANKRUPTCY, DEFAULT

DEFAULT
A euphemism for BANKRUPTCY used in cases when a CORPORATION or GOVERNMENT goes bust. When it's you who is broke, it's still called personal BANKRUPTCY; no euphemisms.

DEFICIT *(of government budget)*
1. If a private company runs a deficit budget, it's called a loss. If a GOVERNMENT runs a deficit, it's called an EXPANSIVE FISCAL POLICY.
2. A small (or sometimes not so small) step towards massive GOVERNMENT DEBT.

DEFLATION *(of consumer prices)*
Negative INFLATION or a decline in the consumer PRICE index. Comes in two varieties:
1. Deflation caused by a growth in productivity and a decline in costs and by an intense degree of COMPETITION: the benign variety.
2. PRICE deflation caused by a collapse of the MONEY supply and subsequent CREDIT CRUNCH. The bad sort of deflation, which often accompanies a CRISIS.
   Alas, there are more than a few inept ACADEMIC ECONOMISTS and half-baked CENTRAL BANKERS who tend to confuse these two very distinct meanings.
See INFLATION

DEFLATION *(of money supply, credit)*

There is less MONEY in the economy when there is a BANKING CRISIS. PEOPLE have less to spend, CORPORATIONS cut JOBS, BANKS operate a CREDIT CRUNCH. This is likely to be accompanied by the DEFLATION of consumer PRICES. Monetary or CREDIT deflation is a big problem. See INFLATION

DEFLATION SPIRAL

A monster that haunts ACADEMIC ECONOMISTS and CENTRAL BANKERS. But what is it? In the words of one CENTRAL BANK:

"DEFLATION has historically been proved to create problems. When there is deflation, future PRICES will be lower than today's PRICES. As it will be cheaper in the future, households wait until PRICES have fallen before they consume. Companies postpone INVESTMENTS until PRICES have fallen. This means that production can fall as long as there is deflation. It may be difficult to break such a deflation process."

This CENTRAL BANK has got it all wrong. It is true that DEFLATION has historically been associated with economic RECESSIONS or DEPRESSIONS. It usually occurs, however, when PEOPLE do not have enough MONEY to spend and CORPORATIONS have no MONEY to invest, buy material or hire workers. Price DEFLATION is thus the effect rather than the cause of a banking or economic CRISIS.

In actual fact, households never postpone CONSUMPTION; otherwise they would have to wait until PRICES had fallen. Would you postpone buying food, drink, electricity, gas, clothes, shoes, TVs, fridges or whatever just because it may be one or two per cent cheaper in a year's time? Of course not. In fact, many households borrow MONEY and pay INTEREST RATES in double-digit figures.

The CENTRAL BANKERS' and ACADEMIC ECONOMISTS' favourite theory of the maleficent deflation spiral is thus plainly wrong. It's against common sense and even against economic theory (proper economic theory, not that taught by most ACADEMIC ECONOMISTS).
See SPURIOUS CORRELATION

DEGREES *(academic)*

A signal that you have sacrificed a great deal of your life to earn some strange abbreviations such as BA, MA, MBA or PhD to add to your name thus enabling you to apply for a JOB in a CORPORATION or BANK without any guarantee you will actually get it, of course. An academic degree allows you to teach in a university and produce more useless ACADEMICS with degrees just like yours.

DEGROWTH

A favourite sour-grapes mental strategy of losers. If you can't achieve ECONOMIC GROWTH and PROSPERITY, pretend you don't need it. See ZERO-GROWTH

DEMOCRACY

1. A system under which VOTERS pretend to believe the promises of POLITICIANS and POLITICIANS pretend to honour their promises.

2. The rule of the many.

3. An excuse used by POLITICIANS, usually in THIRD-WORLD COUNTRIES, to explain why they can't behave decently: *"It's democracy, so don't complain about whoever it was you elected."*

See ELECTIONS, POLITICIANS

Notable & Quotable

"OLIGARCHY is when men of PROPERTY have the GOVERNMENT in their hands; DEMOCRACY, the opposite, when the indigent, and not the men of PROPERTY, are the rulers." (Aristotle, POLITICS, Book III)

"It has been said that DEMOCRACY is the worst form of GOVERNMENT except all the others that have been tried." (Sir Winston CHURCHILL)

"DEMOCRACY is a political system that allows choosing your dictators, after they've told you what they think it is you want to hear." (Anon.)

DENTIST

An example of a useful profession (unlike 'MAINSTREAM economist').

Notable & Quotable

"If economists could manage to get themselves thought of as humble, competent PEOPLE on a level with dentists, that would be splendid." (John Maynard KEYNES)

DEPRECIATION *(of currency)*

A decline in the VALUE of a local CURRENCY expressed in foreign CURRENCIES, caused by market forces and fluctuations. See DEVALUATION

DEPOSIT INSURANCE

Just deposit your MONEY in a BANK and stop worrying, it's insured. And no, you don't have to check the BANK out to see if it is sound or not.
See MORAL HAZARD, BANK RUN

DERIVATIVES

1. Financial weapons of mass destruction.
2. Contracts or SECURITIES whose price is derived from the price of other SECURITIES, COMMODITIES or CURRENCIES, usually involving time, INTEREST RATES, and a lot of unfathomable FINANCIAL MATHEMATICS that is impenetrable even to the BANK MANAGERS who decide about derivative trades.
3. The modern equivalent of thimblerig (the three shells and a pea game): clients have zero chance of understanding the valuation of derivative-based FINANCIAL PRODUCTS.
See OPTIONS, BLACK-SCHOLES MODEL

DESIRE

1. A strong feeling of wanting to have something or wishing for something to happen (Oxford English Dictionary).
2. The engine of ECONOMIC GROWTH.

Notable & Quotable
"Man is the only animal whose desires increase as they are fed; the only animal that is never satisfied." (Henry George)

DETAILS

Cosy places where the devil loves to dwell. Hint: always read the small print.

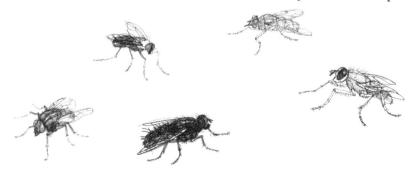

DETROIT
BANKRUPT city in Illinois with half the population it had in the 1950's; metropolitan area with beautifully affordable housing. A house for a dollar sounds like a dream, but is, in fact, a nightmare.
See LONDON, PROPERTY

Curious Fact: Extremely cheap PROPERTIES *in Detroit*
As the financial CRISIS hit Detroit, housing PRICES dropped to absurdly low levels. As of January 2014, eighteen homes in Detroit were listed for $100 or less, with six PROPERTIES listed at $100 and nine at just $1. The rest were listed at various amounts in between, from $50 to $80. You wouldn't be able to resist it, would you...

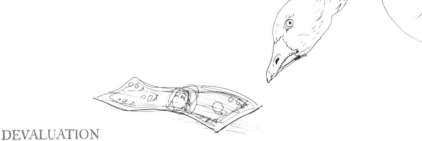

DEVALUATION
1. A decline in the VALUE of a local CURRENCY expressed in foreign CURRENCIES caused by the decision of an authority (GOVERNMENT or CENTRAL BANK).
See DEPRECIATION
2. An indirect form of the partial confiscation of SAVINGS and income in a local CURRENCY.

DEVELOPED *(markets, countries, economies)*
Formerly known as first-world countries; WEALTHY enough that their citizens often prefer living on WELFARE to working and often for that very reason burdened with huge amounts of DEBT in the form of GOVERNMENT BONDS. Economies which are heavily taxed in order to pay for the WELFARE and DEBT service. At a certain point, DEVELOPED markets become too heavily taxed to produce almost anything other than PUBLIC SERVICES. Production is then outsourced to EMERGING MARKETS and SAVINGS deposited in offshore TAX havens.

DEVELOPING COUNTRIES

An obsolete term used from the early 1950's to the late 1980's when it became obvious that most developing countries have never actually DEVELOPED anything other than huge amounts of foreign DEBT. Replaced by the term EMERGING MARKETS.

DISMAL SCIENCE, *The*
ECONOMICS

Notable & Quotable

The phrase "the DISMAL SCIENCE" first occurred in Thomas Carlyle's 1849 tract (somewhat unsympathetically) entitled Occasional Discourse on the Negro Question. The term was meant as the antithesis of the phrase "gay science", which referred to life-enhancing knowledge. The fact that ECONOMICS assumed that PEOPLE were equally deserving of liberty was so offensive to Carlyle that he called ECONOMICS *"the DISMAL SCIENCE"*.

ECONOMICS was dismal for *"finding the secret of this Universe in 'supply and demand,' and reducing the duty of human governors to that of letting men alone."*

Instead, the *"idle Black man in the West Indies"* should be *"compelled to work as he was fit, and to do the Maker's will who had constructed him."* Carlyle also argued for the reintroduction of slavery as a means of regulating the LABOUR market in the West Indies.

It is of course utterly shameful to leave PEOPLE alone and without compulsion or coercion. Quelle horreur.

DICTATORSHIP

A form of GOVERNMENT which limits the RIGHTS of citizens in the name of the COMMON GOOD; it is the dictator who decides what the COMMON GOOD is.
See COMMUNISM, SOCIALISM, MUST, NATIONAL SOCIALISM

DIVERSIFICATION

In finance, diversification means reducing risk by investing in a variety of assets.
In SEX, diversification means increasing risk and expenditure.
See PORTFOLIO, MISTRESS,

DIVORCE

One of the major sources of revenue for lawyers. Fees paid to divorce lawyers improve GDP as they are a part of aggregate private CONSUMPTION.

DIVORCE RATE

An indicator of an improving economy.

Curious Fact: DIVORCES *help the economy*

Bloomberg News, 18 February 2014. The number of Americans getting divorced rose for the third year in a row to about 2.4 million in 2012, after plunging in the 18-month RECESSION ended June 2009, according to US Census Bureau data. Whatever the social and emotional impact, the broad economic effects of the increase are clear: it is contributing to the formation of new households, boosting demand for housing, appliances and furnishings, and spurring the economy. DIVORCES are also prompting more women to enter the LABOUR force. That's all great, then.

DOMINO EFFECT

A kind of chain reaction which occurs when a CRISIS for one BANK drags its counterpart BANKS into CRISIS. A very dangerous state of affairs as most BANKS are inseparably linked to each other. (Very few PEOPLE realise just how fragile the modern banking system is...)

DOT.COM MANIA

The period 1999–2000, when otherwise thoughtful clear-headed PEOPLE convinced themselves that a fledgling internet company with negligible revenues and abysmal losses may have as much VALUE as, say, Boeing, Coca-Cola, Procter & Gamble, Wal-Mart or other such mature businesses.
See EFFICIENT MARKET HYPOTHESIS

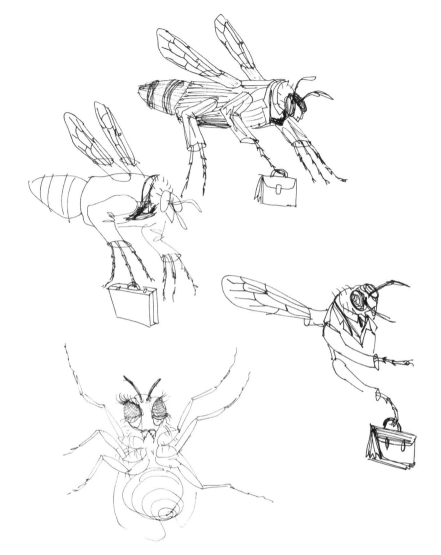

DRONES
1. Male bees who do no real work other than transferring their genetic information.
2. Most employees in banking, finance, POLITICS and academia who do no real work other than transferring financial information (or disinformation).

DSGE MODELS

1. Dynamic Stochastic General EQUILIBRIUM methodology attempts to explain aggregate economic phenomena—such as ECONOMIC GROWTH, BUSINESS CYCLES, and the effects of MONETARY and FISCAL POLICY—on the basis of macroeconomic MODELS derived from microeconomic principles. One of the main reasons macroeconomists seek to build micro-founded MODELS is that, unlike more traditional macroeconometric FORECASTING MODELS, micro-founded MODELS should not, in principle, be vulnerable to the Lucas critique that it is naïve to try to predict the effects of a change in economic policy entirely on the basis of relationships observed in historical data, especially highly aggregated historical data. Furthermore, since the micro-foundations are based on the preferences of the decision-makers in the MODEL, DSGE MODELS feature a natural BENCHMARK for evaluating the WELFARE effects of policy changes. At least that's what Wikipedia says.

2. According to actual experience, being unable to produce any useful forecasts, DSGE is shunned by BANKS and the private sector. It has, however, proven useful as a subject for doctoral theses, working papers and articles for journals recognised by scientists. As such, DSGE is exclusively used by ACADEMIC ECONOMISTS.

3. Academic nonsense invented by DRONES for DRONES.

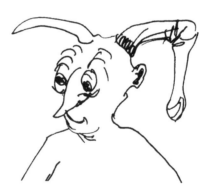

Notable & Quotable
"Like a fire station that automatically burns down whenever a big fire starts, DSGEs become unreliable when they are most needed."
(David F. Hendry, Professor of ECONOMICS, Oxford University, and Grayham E. Mizon, University of Southampton: *Why DSGEs crash during* CRISES. Published at www.voxeu.org, 18 June 2014)

EASTERN EUROPE
Political label that is usually hated by the nations it may apply to. Except for RUSSIA, which is in fact a country that is more Asian than European.

ECONOMICS
A quasi-religious belief system based upon the lunatic notion of the human as a rational being.

ECONOMIC GROWTH
The continuous growth of CONSUMPTION, INVESTMENTS and trade, which should, in theory, bring about PROSPERITY, thereby making you happier.
See GDP, DEGROWTH, ZERO GROWTH

ECONOMIC SCIENCE
1. One of the most important and well-recognised SOCIAL SCIENCES, which involves extensive use of mathematics and enjoys its own NOBEL PRIZE.
2. A textbook example of a 'contradictio in adjecto'.

ECONOMETRICS
FORECASTING done scientifically. Useful for creating JOBS at universities and in various GOVERNMENT institutions but otherwise serves no practical purpose. See DSGE MODELS

EDUCATION
1. Something valuable that remains even when you renounce your DEGREES and burn your diplomas.
2. An elaborate term for the wasted years of youth.
3. STATE-sponsored brainwashing.

EFFICIENT MARKET HYPOTHESIS

The belief that STOCK MARKET ANALYSTS perfectly evaluate all of the available information. You can always rely, therefore, on the market price of ASSETS such as BONDS, EQUITIES or PROPERTY; ANALYSTS are thus expendable and speculative BUBBLES never appear. Unfortunately, the efficient market hypothesis does not solve its own internal theoretical conflict that ANALYSTS are at one and the same time both essential and expendable. This didn't, however, prevent Sveriges Riksbank from awarding the pseudo NOBEL PRIZE to Eugene FAMA. See DOT.COM MANIA, TULIP MANIA

ELECTIONS

A special kind of market. Voters exchange their political POWER for the promises of POLITICIANS every four or five years. Less stable countries require more frequent elections in order to provide their PEOPLE with the illusion that they enjoy a greater level of DEMOCRACY.

EMERGING MARKETS

1. Countries impoverished by long-lasting and inept ECONOMIC policies, but now expected to make a successful U-turn in order to please INVESTORS from DEVELOPED MARKETS. For this reason, often considered INVESTMENT opportunities with plenty of room for ECONOMIC GROWTH.

2. Countries which have been in deep trouble for many years, and certainly not without reason.

See CHINA, DEVELOPED MARKETS, SUBOPTIMAL EQUILIBRIUM

"There's a faint sense of embarrassment and foot-shuffling about the term 'emerging' in particular, because it sounds so patronizing, like the school prizes for 'most improved'. Or the only prize ever won during her school career by the late Princess Diana, an award for the best-kept hamster."
(John Lanchester: *How to Speak* MONEY: *What the* MONEY PEOPLE *say—and what they really mean*)

Curious Fact: GREECE *downgraded*
Countries are rarely downgraded from DEVELOPED to emerging status. GREECE was downgraded in 2013 after several years of professional assistance from the International Monetary Fund, the EUROPEAN UNION, and the European CENTRAL BANK.

ENTITLEMENTS
Benefits paid to one group of VOTERS by POLITICIANS with OTHER PEOPLE'S MONEY. Entitlements usually masquerade as RIGHTS. See HANDOUTS, LIBERALS

Notable & Quotable
"Teach a man to fish and he will eat for life. Give him someone else's fish and he will vote for you." (Anon.)

ENVY

1. The most sincere emotion many PEOPLE are capable of.
2. A major influence on FISCAL POLICIES.
3. One of the sins explicitly proscribed by the Ten Commandments, although few Christians realise this.

See SOCIALISM, PHYSICS ENVY

ENVY TAX

A high marginal income TAX rate, the main purpose of which is to decrease the level of ENVY experienced by VOTERS with below AVERAGE INCOME.

Devil's Question: Will a leftist professor pay the high TAXES he himself proposes?

ENVY is a powerful emotion which always sells very well. At the time of writing, a book completely dedicated to ENVY and the ENVY TAX ranks No. 1 in the Amazon.com list of bestsellers. With a title that evokes Karl MARX ('CAPITAL in the Twenty-First Century'), the book by Professor Thomas Piketty gained instant popularity among SOCIALISTS of all colours and flavours. The central argument of the book is that CAPITAL RETURNS provide systematically higher income than earnings from LABOUR; the world will eventually, therefore, be owned by a handful of CAPITALISTS and the impoverished masses will have nothing to lose but their fetters.

Piketty does not propose income TAX cuts to alleviate the plight of the working classes. Instead, he proposes steeply progressive TAXATION on the rich. 'The rich' are defined as anyone earning over $200,000 a year. The TAX rate for the super-rich (those who earn more than $500,000—the mind boggles) would be as high as 80 per cent.

Neither Professor Piketty nor his admirers seem to be bothered by the likely outcome that a TAX structure like this would severely undermine INVESTMENTS, GROWTH and employment, as it has indeed already done many times in many countries. (See INDIA)

To date, it is not known what Piketty would do with the abundant royalties he is going to make from his bestselling book. If he practised what he preached, he would give most of them to the GOVERNMENT in the form of a voluntary TAX.

"But so successful was this venture that Magrathea itself soon became the richest planet of all time and the rest of the Galaxy was reduced to abject POVERTY. *And so the system broke down, the Empire collapsed, and a long sullen silence settled over a billion worlds, disturbed only by the pen scratchings of scholars as they labored into the night over smug little treaties on the* VALUE *of a planned political economy."*
(Douglas Adams foresaw Piketty in his awesome story of *The Hitchhiker's Guide to the Galaxy*!)

EQUILIBRIUM
A state of affairs in which opposing economic forces (such as supply and demand) are balanced. Forces such as GOVERNMENT intervention, regulation or SUBSIDIES may lead to a SUBOPTIMAL EQUILIBRIUM.

EQUITIES
Equities or common stocks are shares in publicly traded CORPORATIONS, whose price is publicly known, but whose VALUE may be subject to the wildest speculation.

"A cynic is a man who knows the PRICE *of everything and the* VALUE *of nothing."*
(Oscar Wilde understood this, although it is uncertain whether he speculated with EQUITIES himself.)

EURO
1. The common CURRENCY used by the member STATES of the EMU (Economic and Monetary Union, aka the EUROZONE). Introduced in the late 1990's as a means towards economic cooperation, ever closer INTEGRATION, and as a sturdy shield against economic and financial CRISES.
2. An experiment which broke the rules of the OPTIMUM CURRENCY AREA and has shown the theory to have been correct.

EUROPE
A very diverse continent united by ENVY and mutual distaste.

EUROPEAN ECONOMIC COMMUNITY (EEC)
Also known as the Common Market, the EEC worked from 1958 to 1993 as the precursor of the EUROPEAN UNION. If judged according to the idea that the opening of borders for INTERNATIONAL TRADE prevents TRADE WARS and WORLD WARS, the EEC was a huge success.

EUROPEAN UNION

The largest economic experiment ever organised. Since its launch in 1993, it has shown that:

(a) the rate of ECONOMIC GROWTH decreases as the rate of economic INTEGRATION increases, along with UNEMPLOYMENT;

(b) SUBSIDIES are seriously harmful;

(c) Cyril Northcote PARKINSON was right.

As the experiment has involved experimenters, it is unlikely to be finished any time soon.

See BUREAUCRACY

EUROZONE
The group of European countries which share a common CURRENCY, the EURO, which only goes to show that a single MONETARY POLICY can be wrong for all member STATES.

EUTHANASIA OF THE RENTIER
A policy of the SOCIALISATION of INVESTMENTS through high INFLATION accompanied by low INTEREST RATES, which would eventually eliminate the real income of rentiers who own FIXED-INCOME SECURITIES. Advocated by John Maynard KEYNES and implemented by most CENTRAL BANKS in DEVELOPED COUNTRIES. See OUT OF THIN AIR, EXPANSIVE MONETARY POLICY

EXPANSIVE FISCAL POLICY
Profligate spending beyond one's means with the hope of kick-starting ECONOMIC GROWTH. See GOVERNMENT DEBT, RESTRICTIVE FISCAL POLICY

EXPANSIVE MONETARY POLICY

1. The CENTRAL BANK cuts INTEREST RATES, which, in theory, should spur the growth of both CREDIT and CONSUMPTION. This, in turn, stimulates ECONOMIC GROWTH and possibly INFLATION.

2. The CENTRAL BANK cuts INTEREST RATES, which, in fact, means that savers and INVESTORS who own BONDS receive less interest income, and thus spend less; this may cause a RECESSION and possibly DEFLATION.

3. A licence to print MONEY; a priceless item on the BALANCE SHEET.

4. Authorised large-scale FORGERY.

See RESTRICTIVE MONETARY POLICY, EXPANSIVE FISCAL POLICY

EXPERIENCE

The only BUSINESS SCHOOL that really counts.

EXPROPRIATION

According to COMMUNISM and the RADICAL political left, an essential tool for building a better world. See TAXATION, COMMUNISM, NATIONAL SOCIALISM, REAL SOCIALISM, MARXISM

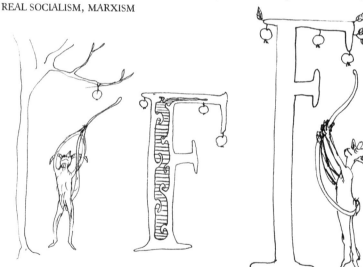

FABIAN SOCIETY

An organisation based on the belief that CAPITALISM can be more reliably and thoroughly destroyed by gradual means than by a SOCIALIST REVOLUTION. It almost succeeded in INDIA and other DEVELOPING COUNTRIES, where Fabian ideas were practised after gaining INDEPENDENCE from GREAT BRITAIN.

FASCISM

A CAPITALIST economy ruled by a totalitarian STATE. Unlike in REAL SOCIALISM, CAPITAL is not fully owned by the GOVERNMENT, but CAPITALISTS are under constant control by, and threat from, the ruling fascist STATE machinery.
See NATIONAL SOCIALISM

Notable & Quotable
"All within the STATE, *nothing outside the state, nothing against the* STATE.*"*
(Benito Mussolini)

Devil's Question: Is FASCISM *right-wing or left-wing?*
This is a subject of endless discussion on the Internet. First of all, there is a difference between fascism and NATIONAL SOCIALISM. The difference is not merely superficial.

For example, FASCISM was not originally formed as an anti-Semitic movement. FASCISM was undoubtedly a totalitarian doctrine, but there were different varieties. Mussolini's version of FASCISM bore certain characteristics of the political left, especially GOVERNMENT involvement in the economy on many levels including agricultural policies, housing policies, public works, PRICE controls, and the all-pervasive collectivism.

The Spanish version of FASCISM implemented by the dictator Francisco Franco (in POWER from 1939 to his death in 1975) was more conservative than Italian FASCISM. Franco, a devout Roman Catholic and Spanish patriot, laid great emphasis on the basic pillars of STATE POWER, particularly the army, the police and the church. Until the 1960's, he pursued no real economic policies other than self-sufficiency and the erection of TRADE BARRIERS. By that time, Spanish workers had started to ask the uneasy question as to why their wages were roughly one third of those enjoyed by workers in GERMANY. Only then did his aides unleash ECONOMIC reforms leading to a more open and less straightjacketed economy.

In short, there were LEFTIST fascist dictators and CONSERVATIVE fascist dictators; both were enemies of freedom. However, to make things even less black-and-white, Franco's fascist GOVERNMENT remained neutral during WWII and saved many Jewish lives. Should Franco be respected as a kind of Spanish Oskar Schindler?

NB: Despite the propaganda and popular wisdom, Hitler was not a FASCIST. *He was a* NATIONAL SOCIALIST, *which is quite different.*

FAT CATS
Popular jargon for obscenely overpaid BANKERS and managers.

Curious Question: Why are FAT CATS *so fat?*
BANKERS and managers have always enjoyed handsome salaries. However, the ratio of executive-to-worker pay at the big British BANKS often exceeds a factor of 100. According to the Financial Times, Barclays pays its chief executive 181 times more than the average worker, and Lloyds 125 times as much. These extremely high salaries, bonuses and 'golden parachutes' are a relatively recent phenomenon, dating back only to the 1990's. Why is this?

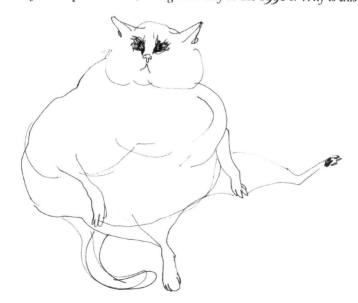

Opinions differ, but MORAL HAZARD is probably the most likely explanation. Managers' salaries began to be tied to performance in the 1990's, according to then-popular management theories. If the company you manage makes a lot of MONEY, you'll receive a share of the profits. On the other hand, if the company loses MONEY, you can still keep your basic salary. You may be fired, but your VALUE in the JOB market increases: the BANKRUPTCY you caused counts as experience!

With the rules set like this, managers are tempted to take more RISKS than they otherwise might. And reckless managers take lots of RISKS. Remember Lehman Brothers.

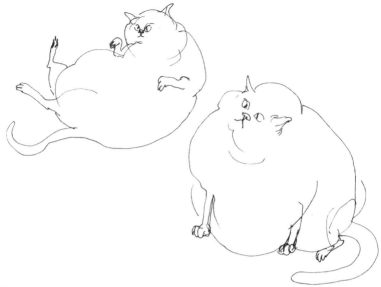

Then the question arises as to whether the GOVERNMENT should do something about it. But before you answer "yes, of course it should", please remember one thing. If the GOVERNMENT starts to meddle in the highest salaries, chances are it won't stop there. Other salaries are going to become progressively taxed, including yours. Ultimately, any crusade against the undeserved benefits of the fat cats will turn against you, even if you (and your family income) are relatively lean.

This is why the Swiss refused GOVERNMENT regulation of top manager salaries in a referendum. The Swiss probably know it's more important to limit GOVERNMENT POWER than to fight against the excessively high benefits of a handful of overpaid BOSSES.

FED

1. The Federal Reserve System is the CENTRAL BANK of the UNITED STATES OF AMERICA, and consists of thirteen Federal Reserve Banks serving twelve Federal Reserve Districts, all of which are under the authority of the politically independent Federal Open Market Committee (FOMC), which is responsible for MONETARY POLICY in the USA.

2. An opaque network of semi-private BANKS whose shareholders may not, however, vote in shareholder meetings and have no right to participate in a BANK's profits. The whole system comes under the authority of the politically unaccountable FOMC, which is responsible for blowing BUBBLES and organising BANK BAILOUTS when the BUBBLES burst.

Curious Question: Is the Federal Reserve public or private?
Is the Fed owned by the GOVERNMENT or by private entities? The answer is not completely straightforward. It's true that the shares of individual Federal Reserve BANKS are held by commercial banks from their respective districts. If you open up a new BANK in Atlanta, the BANK becomes a member BANK of the Federal Reserve BANK of Atlanta. Your BANK must buy shares in the FRB Atlanta, even if you do not want to.

It is also true that the shares come without voting rights and that claims on DIVIDENDS are limited. Private commercial BANKS have no chance of influencing MONETARY POLICY, which is conducted by the FOMC.

So is the FED public or private? It is in fact a quasi-GOVERNMENT agency which contains elements of both the private sector and Federal GOVERNMENT control. Neither fish nor fowl. However, it is certainly not run by the Rothschilds or a handful of super-WEALTHY Jewish families as maintained by certain conspiracy theorists.

FEDERALISM *(federative states)*
A form of GOVERNMENT based upon the redistribution of TAX WEALTH among member STATES so that each of them feels worse off; an additional layer of costs and BUREAUCRACY is another feature of federations. See UNITARY GOVERNMENT

FINANCIAL FREEDOM
An idea for which PEOPLE are willing to slave for 12 or more hours a day, 7 days a week. See MORTGAGE

FINANCIAL PANIC
Catastrophic mood among TRADERS and AMATEUR INVESTORS (and even BANKERS) after discovering once again that the theory of a GREATER FOOL doesn't hold, and that the MINSKY MOMENT has arrived. See BANK RUN

Notable & Quotable
"Panics do not destroy CAPITAL; *they merely reveal the extent to which it has been previously destroyed by its betrayal in hopelessly unproductive works."* (John Mills)

FINANCIAL PRODUCT
A contract between a CLIENT and a BANK which is always profitable for the BANK.

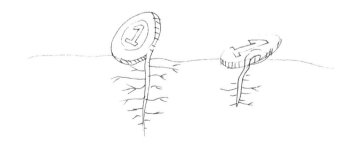

FINE
"A fine is a TAX for doing wrong. A TAX is a fine for doing well."
(Sara Wright, @SaraWright89)

FISCAL POLICY
1. Tool for smoothing the BUSINESS CYCLE by way of increasing or cutting TAX RATES or PUBLIC EXPENDITURE; largely inefficient and even counterproductive.
2. Elaborate theory relating to the extraction of as much MONEY as possible from the economically active part of the population; ideological excuse for perpetually increasing TAX rates.
See ENVY

FIXED-INCOME SECURITIES
Originally BONDS, notes, treasury bills. Now either zero-income SECURITIES OR HIGH-YIELD BONDS. See EUTHANASIA OF THE RENTIER

FLAT TAX
Bizarre idea that the amount of TAXES paid should be proportional to a taxpayer's income. See PROGRESSIVE TAXATION

FORGERY
Unauthorised expansion of the monetary base. See EXPANSIVE MONETARY POLICY

FORECASTING
Futile endeavour based upon extrapolating the past into the future. Usually performed by ANALYSTS and ECONOMISTS in BANKS and research organisations. See BUSINESS CYCLE, ECONOMETRICS, EFFICIENT MARKET HYPOTHESIS

Curious Fact: Swedish central BANK *fails to forecast the economy*
Riksbank, the Swedish CENTRAL BANK—incidentally, the oldest CENTRAL BANK in the world—awards the annual NOBEL PRIZE for ECONOMIC SCIENCES. What institution should know more about ECONOMIC forecasting? Yet in December 2008, after the collapse of Lehman Brothers, Fannie Mae and the like, it foresaw only a mild RECESSION for Sweden amounting to a 0.5 per cent decline in GDP in 2009. In fact, the Swedish economy took a dive by 5.0 per cent that year. A tenfold difference.

This wasn't the only mistake made by Riksbank. In December 2007, when it was quite clear that STOCK MARKETS were tumbling worldwide and something was going seriously wrong, its GDP forecast for 2008 amounted to a rosy 2.4 per cent growth. (The reality was a 0.6 per cent decline.) There was, on the other hand, a 6.6 per cent BOOM in 2010, which the Riksbank failed to forecast. (Its prediction for 2010 was 2.7 per cent growth.)

Cold comfort can be found in the fact that other CENTRAL BANKS and ACADEMIC ECONOMISTS across the world fared similarly poorly in terms of their forecasting POWER. Sometimes much worse. And the moral is? Forecasting fails most spectacularly when you need it most desperately.

FRACTIONAL BANKING
A modern system of banking. While early in their history BANKS had to cover the VALUE of deposits by their reserves, these currently stand at just less than 1/10. The rest is covered by good hope and INTERBANK MARKET operations. A banking CRISIS starts when good hope (and interbank market LIQUIDITY) evaporates. See BANKS, BAILOUT

FRIEDMAN, *Milton*

An economist who gained his fame (and a pseudo NOBEL PRIZE) for stating the bleeding obvious: (1) private owners usually take better care of their possessions than do PUBLIC SERVANTS of public PROPERTY; (2) printing lots of MONEY brings about high INFLATION; (3) playing with TAX rates is too clumsy a tool for fine-tuning the BUSINESS CYCLE. As he was accustomed to telling the uncomfortable truth, many POLITICIANS have hated him well beyond his grave.

Notable & Quotable
"The two greatest enemies of free enterprise in the UNITED STATES ... *have been, on the one hand, my fellow intellectuals and, on the other hand, the business* CORPORATIONS *of this country."* (Milton FRIEDMAN)

FUNDAMENTAL ANALYSIS

A somewhat naïve belief that annual reports and financial statements of publicly traded companies contain useful information on the future movements of EQUITY PRICES. See ANALYST, EFFICIENT MARKETS

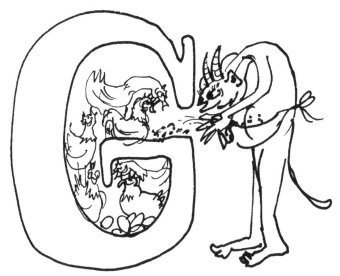

GAMBLING INDUSTRY

A business which collects MONEY from PEOPLE in exchange for hope. Unlike when you pay TAXES, there is at least a minuscule chance of winning.
See INSURANCE, LOTTERY

GDP

1. Gross Domestic Product is the sum of private CONSUMPTION, GOVERNMENT CONSUMPTION, CAPITAL INVESTMENTS and net exports, which totally disregards the quality of private CONSUMPTION, the purposefulness of GOVERNMENT CONSUMPTION, the rate of return on INVESTMENTS, and profits from exports.
2. A measure of the size of an economy; not a measure of PROSPERITY.
3. The modern equivalent of the golden calf.

The Devil Is In The Detail: GDP = C + G + I + NX, where

C ... CONSUMPTION, which means more cars competing for parking spaces, more clothes in your wife's wardrobe, more toys all over the floor to keep treading on, and more fat on your tummy and cholesterol in your veins.
G ... GOVERNMENT CONSUMPTION; yet more wasteful spending by BUREAUCRATS. Note that the idle recipients of WELFARE, who are allowed to sleep in their beds while you go about your daily grind, are accounted for as part of C.
I ... CAPITAL INVESTMENTS, which may mean your eventual replacement by a robot.
NX ... NET EXPORTS, usually a huge negative figure, which means more low quality imports from countries we won't mention for fear of accusations of political incorrectness, more CONSUMPTION, and a shrinking domestic manufacturing sector.

Curious Fact: Drugs and PROSTITUTION *as valuable as agriculture in the British* GDP

Under EU rules, GREAT BRITAIN will add illegal drug sales and PROSTITUTION to its calculation of GDP. The GOVERNMENT's statistics watchdog is set to confirm that Britain makes £10 billion a year from drug dealers and SEX WORKERS. The Office for National Statistics was expected to comply with new EUROPEAN UNION rules by revealing its initial estimates of the size of these illegal industries (and how it made the calculation) as early as March 2014. According to The Telegraph, £5.3 billion was attributable to PROSTITUTION while illegal drugs were worth £4.4 billion. Together, they amount to around 0.7 per cent of the UK economy, or roughly the same amount as agriculture. Other illegal activities, such as the smuggling of alcohol and tobacco, are already included in UK growth and make up some £300 million.

That's quite some improvement.

Notable & Quotable
"It once puzzled me that many economists in the financial sector FORECAST *and discussed* GDP *without knowing what it was. I have since realised the* JOB *of market pundits is not to* FORECAST GDP *but to* FORECAST *what the statistics office will announce is* GDP, *and that is not at all the same."* (John Kay)

GLOBALISATION

The process which can bring you CLIENTS from RUSSIA, INDIA or CHINA, and neighbours from the same nations (and many more). It may also OUTSOURCE your JOB to the said countries. It may, furthermore, make PROPERTY more expensive as your buying power has to compete with eager PROPERTY buyers from RUSSIA, INDIA, and CHINA.

GOLD DIGGER

A woman in search of a wealthy man. A gold digger sees SEX and MARRIAGE as purely financial transactions and thus regards herself as a saleable COMMODITY. See MISTRESS, SEX WORKER

Notable & Quotable

"... what you suggest is a simple trade: you bring your looks to the party and I bring my MONEY. Fine, simple. But here's the rub, your looks will fade and my MONEY will likely continue into perpetuity... in fact, it is very likely that my income increases but it is an absolute certainty that you won't be getting any more beautiful!

So, in economic terms you are a depreciating ASSET and I am an earning ASSET. Not only are you a depreciating ASSET, your depreciation accelerates! Let me explain, you're 25 now and will likely stay pretty hot for the next 5 years, but less so each year. Then the fade begins in earnest. By 35 stick a fork in you!

So in WALL STREET terms, we would call you a trading position, not a BUY AND HOLD... hence the rub... MARRIAGE. It doesn't make good business sense to 'buy you' (which is what you're asking) so I'd rather lease. In case you think I'm being cruel, I would say the following. If my MONEY were to go away, so would you, so when your beauty fades I need an out. It's as simple as that. So a deal that makes sense is dating, not MARRIAGE.

Separately, I was taught early in my career about the EFFICIENT MARKET HYPOTHESIS. *So, I wonder why a girl as 'articulate, classy and spectacularly beautiful' as you has been unable to find your sugar daddy. I find it hard to believe that if you are as gorgeous as you say you are that the $500K hasn't found you, if not only for a tryout."*

(By an anonymous writer, allegedly a WALL STREET BANKER, in reply to a GOLD DIGGER complaining she couldn't find a wealthy husband)

GOLD STANDARD

1. A system of CURRENCY based upon the fixed amount of gold in each unit of MONEY; the best monetary system for avoiding INFLATION.

2. A barbaric relic which caused multiple FINANCIAL CRISES in centuries past; no longer in use. Replaced by fiat CURRENCIES, which allow the MONEY SUPPLY to inflate in a much more straightforward way. Fiat MONEY is a more modern, more efficient cause of BANKING CRISES in EUROPE, too.

See BITCOIN, KEYNES

GOVERNMENT

1. An organised group of PEOPLE who are convinced that they can run the STATE. Sometimes not very well organised, however. In most democratic countries, the GOVERNMENT is appointed by PARLIAMENT. In the USA, GOVERNMENT POWER is vested in the person of the president of the UNITED STATES OF AMERICA, while the cabinet merely has a supporting role.

The American system of GOVERNMENT is clearly superior in the sense that an American voter knows very well that the president is always to blame. The continental European system of mostly coalition GOVERNMENTS with a more balanced distribution of POWER is better at hiding who holds the responsibility. Europeans are usually more confused as to who it is they should point the finger at.

2. In most countries, the single largest borrower and DEBTOR.

See BONDS, INFLATION

"Government has three primary functions. It should provide for military defense of the nation. It should enforce contracts between individuals. It should protect citizens from crimes against themselves or their PROPERTY. *When government in pursuit of good intentions tries to rearrange the economy, legislate morality, or help special interests, the costs come in inefficiency, lack of motivation, and loss of freedom. Government should be a referee, not an active player."* (Milton FRIEDMAN)

"The worst evils that mankind has ever had to endure were inflicted by bad governments." (Ludwig von MISES)

"I don't know why people think the only thing government does is social services. What about war, DEBT, *mass murder, mass* UNEMPLOYMENT, *etc.?"* (Yatish Parmar)

GREAT DEPRESSION *(Recession)*

The name given to any recent economic CRISIS which seems to have been unusually deep and long. To date there have been three CRISES named "Great":

1. The Great Depression of 1873: in the aftermath of this CRISIS, COMMUNISM became popular as the way to end CAPITALIST chaos and install a new order.

2. The Great Depression of the early 1930's: in the aftermath of this CRISIS, NATIONAL SOCIALISM arose in GERMANY as the way to end CAPITALIST chaos and install a new order.

3. The Great RECESSION starting in 2008: after the previous two bad EXPERIENCES, the word "RECESSION" was used rather than "depression". Its aftermath is not quite clear yet, but certain fairly loud voices are demanding an end to CAPITALIST chaos and the beginning of a new order.

GREATER FOOL THEORY

The conviction that no matter how high the PRICE of STOCKS (or COMMODITIES, PROPERTY), there is always a 'greater fool' willing to buy anything at any PRICE, however outlandish it may seem.

GREED

One of the central assumptions ECONOMICS makes about human nature.
See DESIRE

Notable & Quotable
"Well first of all, tell me: Is there some SOCIETY you know that doesn't run on GREED? You think RUSSIA doesn't run on GREED? You think CHINA doesn't run on GREED? What is GREED? Of course, none of us are greedy, it's only the other fellow who's greedy. The world runs on individuals pursuing their separate interests. The great achievements of civilization have not come from GOVERNMENT bureaus. Einstein didn't construct his theory under order from a BUREAUCRAT. Henry Ford didn't revolutionize the automobile industry that way. In the only cases in which the masses have escaped from the kind of grinding POVERTY you're talking about, the only cases in recorded history, are where they have had CAPITALISM and largely free trade. If you want to know where the masses are worse off, worst off, it's exactly in the kinds of societies that depart from that."
(Milton FRIEDMAN)

GROUPTHINK

A way of collective thinking often used in GOVERNMENTS, BANKS, INVESTMENT FUNDS, HEDGE FUNDS and EUROPEAN UNION bodies, which excludes correct conclusions by bullying opponents and suppressing dissenting opinions.

HANDOUTS

ENTITLEMENTS which are completely unearned by their benefactor. Unlike SOCIAL SECURITY—which is at least partly paid for by its recipients—handouts are gifts provided free of charge (or for votes). See LIBERALS

HAPPINESS

1. The feeling that should follow after achieving all of the items in MASLOW'S HIERARCHY OF HUMAN NEEDS, especially a Wi-Fi connection.
2. The absence of stress that is usually associated with accumulating MONEY and spending it on MISTRESSES and LUXURY GOODS.
3. Something you choose to pursue in life; see RIGHTS

Notable & Quotable
"GOVERNMENT*'s first duty is to protect the* PEOPLE, *not run their lives.*"
(Ronald Reagan)

HARROD'S

A place in LONDON where overpriced imported LUXURY GOODS are sold to foreign visitors, thus boosting British ECONOMIC GROWTH and improving VAT statistics. See INTERNATIONAL TRADE

HEDGE FUNDS

1. Unregulated INVESTMENT FUNDS accessible only to ACCREDITED INVESTORS. Hedge funds are supposed to provide higher RETURNS in exchange for a higher RISK. In fact, very often the only thing that materialises is the RISK.
2. The kind of business that is usually set up by fired (but nonetheless still overconfident) CITY BANKERS.

HERD BEHAVIOUR

A wonderful mechanism of mass psychology which transmutes conscious human beings into herd animals. See GROUPTHINK

HIGH-YIELD BONDS

A highly risky category of FIXED-INCOME securities offering high yields, but not always high RETURNS. See RISK-FREE BONDS

HYPE

1. Extravagant or intensive publicity or promotion (Oxford English Dictionary).
2. Phase (d) of the INVESTMENT DECISION CYCLE. See BUBBLE, BRIC

HYPERINFLATION

If consumer prices grow faster than 100 per cent annually, hyperinflation begins. It has always been deliberately caused by CENTRAL BANKS (or POLITICIANS influencing CENTRAL BANKS) with the aim of paying off GOVERNMENT DEBT with worthless DEBASED MONEY. Only stupid GOVERNMENTS, however, use outright hyperinflation. The smarter ones resort to EXPANSIVE MONETARY POLICY or QUANTITATIVE EASING, which is less obvious and maintains the illusion of PRICE stability. See CAPM, INFLATION, HAVENSTEIN

INDEPENDENCE (of CENTRAL BANKS)

1. The purposeful isolation of CENTRAL BANKS from political influence with the primary aim of keeping MONETARY POLICY free from the pressure to print uncovered MONEY in order to pay off GOVERNMENT DEBT. It has been shown that the independence of CENTRAL BANKS usually contributes to lower rates of INFLATION if INFLATION measurement is adequately rigged.

2. Irresponsibility taken to the point of perfection.

See OUT OF THIN AIR

INEQUALITY *(of income and* PROPERTY*)*

An economic variable which is always perceived as too high, especially by the two thirds of the population who suffer below-AVERAGE INCOME.

See AVERAGE EARNINGS, ENVY TAX

Curious Fact: Low income inequality has a dark side

Generally speaking, low inequality is considered good, whereas high inequality means a sharp division between the rich and the poor. It's not that straightforward, however. In 1937, almost 13 per cent of private income was earned by the richest 1 per cent of the British population. At that time, GREAT BRITAIN was prospering and enjoying a period of growth.

Over time, British SOCIETY grew more egalitarian, with the lowest point of inequality occurring in 1976. In that year, the richest percentile earned a fraction over 4 per cent of private income and GREAT BRITAIN was so down and desperate that she had to ask the IMF for help. According to an alternative set of statistics, however, British society was most egalitarian in the years 1978–79. This was the era of the Winter of Discontent, an infamous episode in British history. The share of gross income earned by the extremely rich top 0.1 per cent fell to its lowest level of all time. It was not a good time for the poor or for the middle classes.

As time passed, inequality in GREAT BRITAIN more than doubled, until 2000, when the top percentile's share of income once more exceeded 10 per cent. But inequality cannot be said to be all bad, only extremes of inequality (including extremely low inequality).

Curious Question: What does JAPAN *have in common with the* CZECH REPUBLIC*?*

According to the ratio of income of the richest 10 per cent to the poorest 10 per cent of the population, the most unequal economies are Bolivia, Namibia, Sierra Leone, Guinea-Bissau, and Haiti. None of these countries is a paragon of a virtuous CAPITALIST economy. According to the same measure, the five most egalitarian economies are JAPAN, the CZECH REPUBLIC, Bosnia and Herzegovina, HUNGARY, and Finland; an odd mixture indeed.

You may have spotted that a low level of inequality represents a burden from the past for former COMMUNIST countries. In Scandinavia and JAPAN, however, it is the result of a high TAX burden and a WELFARE STATE. In all countries, both COMMUNIST and CAPITALIST, low inequality has been associated with a slow pace of ECONOMIC GROWTH.

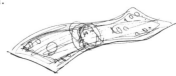

Notable & Quotable

"To endure, a DEMOCRACY, *like an* OLIGARCHY, *needs both the rich and the poor. A* DEMOCRACY *that destroys the well-off becomes unstable. Where the* PEOPLE *have authority over the laws, demagogues tear the city in two by fighting with the rich. Instead, they should do the opposite and appear to speak on the behalf of the rich."* (Aristotle)

"Equality is a slogan based on ENVY. *It signifies: 'Nobody is going to occupy a place higher than I.'"* (Alexis de Tocqueville)

"Common sense is the best distributed ASSET *in the world, for every man is convinced that he is well supplied with it."* (René Descartes)

INFERIORITY COMPLEX

A painful feeling that occurs when a social scientist reads about the achievements of the natural sciences and realises that he or she is not, in fact, a scientist in the strict sense of the word. Different social scientists develop differing adaptive strategies according to their intellectual abilities. Economists produce complex theories stuffed with calculus and algebra. Rather than providing tools for practical analysis, the main purpose of these theories is to raise the profession's self-esteem.

Philosophers and sociologists resort to recycling Hegel or Heidegger, which may, superficially at least, look almost as intellectual as financial mathematics, but doesn't require the knowledge of calculus. See PHYSICS ENVY, DSGE MODELS

INFLATION

1. The gradual increase of the MONEY SUPPLY in the economy.
2. The growth of the CONSUMER PRICE INDEX.
3. A convenient way to tax PEOPLE's SAVINGS and income by debasing the CURRENCY.
4. An indirect subsidy to borrowers, including the GOVERNMENT.
See CURRENCY DEBASEMENT, DEFLATION

Curious Fact: INFLATION *can be your friend*

If you can't beat them, join them. Since you can't beat inflation (unless you're a CENTRAL BANKER) it would appear worthwhile to explore ways of getting along with it.

Inflation is never a friend to FIXED-INCOME INVESTMENTS. You'll be daft to think they were risk-free or even low-risk. To benefit from inflation, one must invest in something whose VALUE is gradually inflated by the growth of MONEY. Hint number one: read the "Curious Fact" below MONEY SUPPLY.

Hint number two: in 1929, there was about $100 billion circulating in the US economy and the Dow Jones index was somewhere around 100 points.

Fifty years later, the US MONEY SUPPLY was at $850 billion while the Dow fluctuated in the 800–890 points band. Thirty years later still, in 2009, the supply of readily available MONEY in the USA went over the $9,500 billion mark, with the Dow swinging from around 8,000 to over 10,000 points.

So, now do you understand how INFLATION can be your friend?

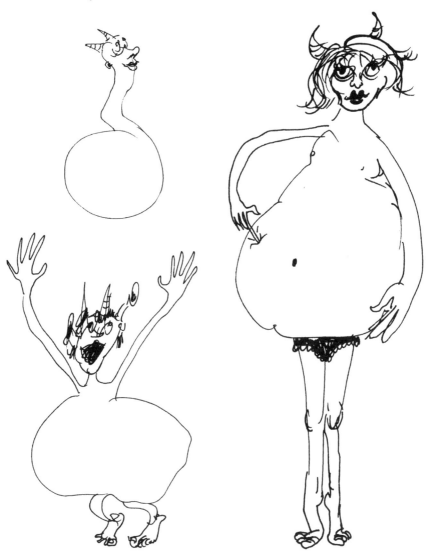

INFLATION RISK

When INFLATION catches unsuspecting INVESTORS unawares, the real VALUE of BONDS may shrink out of sight. Owners of risk-free BONDS are especially vulnerable. (And always remember: there's no such thing as a free lunch.)

Curious Fact: How Britain solved her DEBT *burden, literally*
In the 19th century, the unsuspecting British public was used to zero INFLATION. In fact, on average, consumer PRICES fell very slightly between the end of the Napoleonic WARS and the 1890's. Nothing was safer than British GOVERNMENT BONDS, appropriately called "gilts".

WORLD WAR I was a big blow to British public finance. DEBT service (paying interest alone) took two fifths of British Treasury income. The looming prospect of the principal payment term signalled acute danger for Britain's financial stability.

The GOVERNMENT organised a massive campaign, appealing to British patriotism. It managed to convince the public to exchange 30-year GOVERNMENT BONDS (gilts) issued in 1917 with a coupon rate of 5 per cent issued for consols (BONDS with infinite maturity, which pay only interest and no principal) with a 3.5 per cent coupon rate. This was touted as a good idea.

Indeed it was a good idea—for the Treasury. Between 1932 and 1997, British INFLATION averaged 6 per cent per annum. Not exactly HYPERINFLATION, but still, consumer PRICES rose by a total of 3,408 per cent over that period. And, incidentally, from 1997 to 2012, inflation eroded the purchasing power of the pound by a further third. This was equivalent to annual INFLATION of 2.7 per cent. Not so bad.

RISK-free British gilts became almost worthless as the INFLATION RISK materialised. In 1999, the Financial Times called it a "massive swindle". 'Patriotism' in one era became a 'swindle' in another.

INFLATION TARGETING
The modern approach to MONETARY POLICY, which gives CENTRAL BANKERS an excellent excuse to neglect or ignore developments in the REAL ECONOMY, including the inception of CREDIT BUBBLES and SPECULATIVE BUBBLES.

INTEGRATION *(European)*
1. The removal of barriers to INTERNATIONAL TRADE and INVESTMENTS, the introduction of common standards and rules among member countries, and the introduction of common policies for the fostering of ECONOMIC GROWTH.
2. The gradual growth of central political POWER for the unelected European GOVERNMENT in Brussels at the expense of COMPETITION and COMPETITIVENESS.

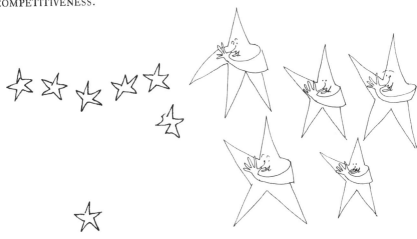

INTELLECTUAL PROPERTY
1. In an economy which is DEVELOPED to the point of being almost completely OUTSOURCED, intellectual PROPERTY is one of the last things to retain its productive potential; the others being the CITY OF LONDON and the Royal Family.
2. Something that requires intellect in order to be valued.

INTERNATIONAL TRADE
A COMPETITION which everybody should win. At least in theory. In practice (as in football), GERMANY always wins.

INSURANCE

A branch of the GAMBLING INDUSTRY which bets on fear. You win when something bad happens to you. The insurance company wins if you are sufficiently frightened. See LIFE INSURANCE

INTEREST GROUPS

Formal or informal associations of CORPORATIONS, trade unions or civic movements of various sorts which aim to influence the decision-making process in the GOVERNMENT or in PARLIAMENT. One of the most powerful interest groups includes members of the GOVERNMENT or PARLIAMENT themselves. The single most important interest group, however, is PUBLIC SERVANTS. See BUREAUCRAT

INTEREST RATE RISK

When INTEREST RATES rise, BOND PRICES fall. INVESTORS who previously bought pricey RISK-FREE BONDS may be rather surprised to see the VALUE of their portfolios plummeting, sometimes at double-digit rates. See INFLATION RISK

INTEREST RATES

The interest rate is the PRICE of DEBT. It may differ considerably, depending on circumstances:

1. If you are a depositor (i.e., you lend your MONEY to a BANK), you usually get a minuscule nominal rate that does not even keep pace with consumer PRICE INFLATION.

2. If you are a debtor, you pay a large amount to cover the costs of your BANK, its PROFITS, and the FAT CAT salaries of its MANAGERS.

INVESTMENT

The action or process of investing MONEY for PROFIT, or so says the Oxford English Dictionary (or for loss, as many experienced INVESTORS may add). See ACTIVE PORTFOLIO MANAGEMENT, BUY-AND-HOLD STRATEGY, RISK, INVESTMENT DECISION CYCLE

Notable & Quotable
"Investing should be more like watching paint dry or watching grass grow. If you want excitement, take $800 and go to Las Vegas." (Paul Samuelson)

INVESTMENT BANK

1. A BANK which specialises in SECURITIES trading. Investment BANKS employ a number of ANALYSTS and TRADERS. When they fail, they become a public LIABILITY, which might result in a BAILOUT.
2. A special form of casino with a more lax regulatory regime than normal commercial BANKS. (Not to mention casinos.)

INVESTMENT DECISION CYCLE

A cycle of actions taken in a certain order by AMATEUR INVESTORS:

(a) Doubt. I'm not sure if investing in EQUITIES is a good idea at all.

(b) Attention. Look, the STOCK MARKET is rising. Perhaps I should buy something.

(c) Attraction. Yes, the market has been rising for a while. Buying stock is definitely a good idea!

(d) Action. I did it and I'm going to be rich soon, even though some stupid BEARS claim that the market is in a BUBBLE phase!

(e) Second thoughts. The market has declined 10 per cent since I invested my entire fortune and my granny's life savings. They're saying it's just a correction. Let's wait and see.

(f) Grave doubts. I'm 30 per cent down, but I'll keep waiting. They say stocks are INVESTMENTS for the long run, so let's hope it is indeed just temporary.

(g) Panic. I'm 50 per cent off and I can't afford to lose the other 50. I'm going to sell my position as the world is melting and I don't believe there will be any form of STOCK MARKET recovery during my lifetime. Away with stocks!

(h) Surrender. I just have to face it. I lost half of the VALUE of my INVESTMENTS. But it wasn't my fault. They lied to me. They lied when they said I should buy EQUITIES. They lied again when they said the world was melting and the market would lose all of its VALUE. Now the STOCK MARKET is back at its pre-crisis level and still growing, but I don't want to hear any more about it. I'll keep the rest of my MONEY in BANK ACCOUNTS or GOVERNMENT BONDS.

NB: Charles Kindleberger presents only five stages in his famous book, 'Manias, Panics and Crashes':
1. Displacement (Doubt, Attention);
2. Euphoria (Attraction);
3. Mania (Action);
4. Distress (Second thoughts, Grave doubts, and Panic); and
5. Revulsion (Surrender).

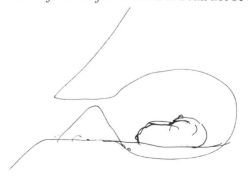

Having met a number of distressed AMATEUR INVESTORS, I felt this point warranted closer attention. See CLIENTS, HYPE

INVESTMENT FUNDS
SECURITIES managed by INVESTMENT MANAGERS as PORTFOLIOS of other SECURITIES with DIVERSIFIED RISK, primarily focused on retail CLIENTS. Although the performance of most funds usually lags behind their BENCHMARK, it is considerably better than what most PEOPLE can make by investing on their own. See RISK, HEDGE FUNDS

INVESTMENT HORIZON
The minimum recommended holding time for riskier types of SECURITIES. INVESTMENT MANAGERS recommend holding on to EQUITIES for at least five years. According to experience, if EQUITY PRICES fall, they usually rise to original levels within a five year period. This does not necessarily hold, however, for most EMERGING MARKETS, such as BRIC, and for JAPAN. In some cases, the minimum investment horizon may outlast your lifetime and still not be enough.

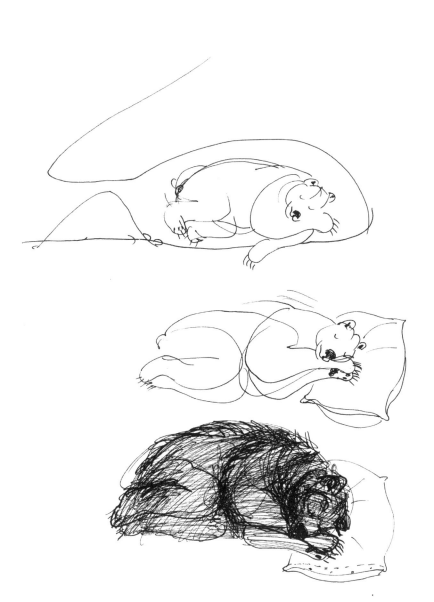

INVESTMENT MANAGERS
Highly skilled and well-paid professionals who rarely beat AVERAGE RETURNS of broad STOCK MARKET indices; still, INVESTMENT managers usually commit fewer costly mistakes than their CLIENTS do when the latter are left unattended at home. See AMATEUR INVESTORS

INVESTOR
An optimist who believes that the world does indeed have a future so it makes sense not to squander all available MONEY right now on SEX and drugs. See AMATEUR INVESTORS

IQ
The most important factor of production, which is wasted and abused more often than any other production factor. Most totalitarian regimes deliberately attempt to eradicate or expel much of their intellectual elite. A lack of intellectual freedom brings about economic stagnation in such regimes. Always. Absolutely always. See HUNGARY, STALIN, LABOUR

Diabolical Question: Do the IQs of nations differ – and if so, why?
Nations naturally differ in their physical characteristics, such as skin colour, average height, or body mass. A truly devilish question would be: do nations differ in their average IQ?

Simply asking the question is inherently dangerous. The notion of a "master race" and "slave races" led to one of the worst tragedies in the history of human civilisation. Few researchers, therefore, have paid serious attention to such a thorny subject.

Richard Lynn and Tatu Vanhanen are an important exception with their controversial book: "IQ and the WEALTH of Nations". The book has often been criticised for a series of methodological issues, such as mixing IQ surveys conducted using different methodologies.

But still, there is reason to believe that national IQs do actually differ and for a somewhat mundane reason: nutrition. In 2004, the United Nations published a report which said that 40 per cent of the population of DEVELOPING COUNTRIES suffers from a lack of iron. According to the study, this can reduce IQ by something like 5 to 7 points. Then there is a lack of iodine. When a pregnant woman has insufficient iodine in her body, her child may suffer irreversible brain damage and could have an IQ that is 10 to 15 points lower than it would otherwise be. According to Nicholas Kristof, a columnist for the New York Times, iodine deficiency may result in a global loss of more than 1 billion IQ points. Kristof adds that until recently, 6 out of 10 Pakistani schoolchildren were iodine-deficient.

The list of important but often deficient micronutrients includes folic acid, vitamin A and niacin. Explaining the difference in IQ between nations does not require a racist worldview. Poor diet is quite enough. (Never underestimate iodine; thank God for fish and chips.)

JOB
You sell your time, brains and skills to a CORPORATION. In return, the CORPORATION provides you with some MONEY and a false sense of security.

KEYNES, *John Maynard*

By far the most abused (and thus the most influential) economist of the 20th century.

See also JOHN MAYNARD KEYNES in the section A PANOPTIC OF LUMINARIES AND THEIR INFAMOUS FINANCIAL FIASCOS

KEYNESIANISM

An optimistic doctrine which holds that the GOVERNMENT can smooth out the BUSINESS CYCLE by using a variety of tools, including, first and foremost, FISCAL POLICY and MONETARY POLICY. Vulgar Keynesianism, much popular among POLITICIANS since Keynes' death in 1946, essentially says that GOVERNMENT DEBT is harmless during your term, and if necessary you can dissolve the real VALUE of GOVERNMENT BONDS by INFLATION.

See JOHN MAYNARD KEYNES, FRIEDMAN, MONEY (fiat), EUTHANASIA OF THE RENTIER

LABOUR

One of the key factors of production. Unlike the other two (LAND and CAPITAL), labour is heavily TAXED in modern economies and therefore systematically overpriced. Seen UNEMPLOYMENT

Curious Fact: LABOUR *is taxed almost as heavily as cigarettes*
If a GOVERNMENT wants to discourage people from consuming alcohol or tobacco, it introduces a consumption TAX (also called excise duty). A high TAX burden on, for example, cigarettes, consequently makes demand for cigarettes fall.

Similarly, if you TAX LABOUR, demand for it will fall. The excise TAX on cigarettes in BELGIUM is 59.5 per cent of the total price. The total TAX burden on labour in the same country is 55.5 per cent (single worker, no children, average wage). Not quite incidentally, unemployment in BELGIUM has been a persistent problem. The same worker would be taxed at only 21 per cent in SWITZERLAND. And yes, UNEMPLOYMENT in SWITZERLAND has traditionally been low.

Notable & Quotable
"Hard work is simply the refuge of PEOPLE *who have nothing whatever to do.*" (Oscar Wilde)
"*I have long been of the opinion that if work were such a splendid thing the rich would have kept more of it for themselves.*" (Bruce Grocott)
"*We have a system that increasingly* TAXES *work and subsidizes non-work.*" (Milton FRIEDMAN)

LABOUR THEORY OF VALUE
A theory which assumes that the VALUE of any good is proportional to the amount of work necessary to produce it. The difference between the market price and the VALUE is called the SURPLUS VALUE. The concept that CAPITALISTS unjustly keep the surplus value is the essence of MARXISM. Labour camps for CAPITALISTS were just the logical consequence of the labour theory of value. Shortages of food, clothes, housing and even toilet paper in Marxist economies were the consequence of a lack of CAPITALISTS. Note that LENIN, STALIN, MAO and POL POT (all of them) were ideologically anchored in the labour theory of VALUE. See MARGINAL THEORY OF VALUE

LAISSEZ-FAIRE
A ridiculous ideology which maintains that humans can live, work, prosper, and even be happy, with little or no interference from the GOVERNMENT.

LAND
Of the three factors of production, land is the one that most WARS are waged over. Few GOVERNMENTS would launch a military conflict simply to attain more workers. See CAPITAL, LABOUR

LAFFER CURVE

An elementary application of calculus in the calculation of TAX revenue as a function of the TAX RATE. It may safely be assumed that a zero TAX RATE YIELDS zero revenue. So much is obvious. A 100 per cent TAX RATE has the same effect, as TAXPAYERS naturally give up working when all of their earnings are confiscated. Much to the chagrin of advocates of high TAXATION, and SOCIALISTS, elementary calculus has proved to be right in many instances. Optimum TAX RATES, however, remain the subject of fierce debate. See CONFISCATORY RATES OF TAXATION, PROGRESSIVE TAXATION

LEADER

The literal English translation of the German word "Führer". See BOSS

LIABILITY

1. A legal responsibility for something.
2. Liabilities in ACCOUNTING: the right-hand side of the BALANCE SHEET; a source of the financing of ASSETS.
3. A MISTRESS whose consumption of LUXURY GOODS exceeds reasonable limits.

LIBERALS

1. In the USA: social democrats or SOCIALISTS; PEOPLE who believe that ENTITLEMENTS or HANDOUTS are civil RIGHTS.
2. In the UK and continental Europe: a bunch of idealistic fools who believe that the STATE could and should be limited in its powers as much as possible; see also CLASSICAL LIBERALS.
See RIGHTS, SOCIALISM, NATIONAL SOCIALISM

LIBERTARIANS

FREEDOM-loving individualists who follow the rule "live and let live." Libertarians have no interest in the STATE. Sadly, this does not prevent the STATE from being interested in libertarians as TAXPAYERS. See LIBERALS, AUSTRIAN SCHOOL

Notable & Quotable
"Disobedience is the true foundation of liberty. The obedient must be slaves."
(Henry David Thoreau)

LIFE INSURANCE
A special sort of betting on the length of your life; you win when you die, to the great delight of your heirs.

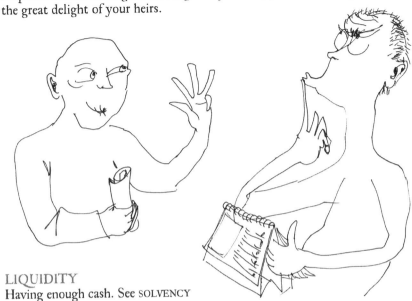

LIQUIDITY
Having enough cash. See SOLVENCY

LOBBYISTS
Representatives of INTEREST GROUPS who assume that political POWER is a tradable COMMODITY. See PEOPLE, PARLIAMENT, POLITICIANS

LONDON
The largest and wealthiest metropolitan area in EUROPE, which goes to show that high GDP per capita often goes hand in hand with surreal PROPERTY PRICES and an influx of immigrants from all over the world.
See DETROIT, OLIGARCHS, COLONIALISM, MIDDLE EAST

LOTTERY
A TAX on PEOPLE who are bad at maths.

LOVE
1. A basic human instinct that urges PEOPLE to form families and sign LIFE INSURANCE policies.
2. The primary driver of the fashion and LUXURY GOODS industries.
See SEX

LUXURY GOODS
Fashion and jewellery. Mostly worn by MISTRESSES when genuine and by SEX WORKERS when fake. See LOVE, SEX

MADE IN CHINA

A label which could be the modern equivalent of MADE IN GERMANY in Victorian times. See TRADE WARS

MADE IN GERMANY

"Bad, valueless. Outcome of the vast quantity of inferior goods imported from GERMANY," according to *Ware's Victorian Dictionary of Slang and Phrase* published in 1909. The label was mandatorily introduced in Britain by the Merchandise Marks Act in 1887 to protect unsuspecting British consumers from shoddy German imports. Over time, it became the hallmark of quality as German manufacturing quality improved. Few PEOPLE now realise its former stigma. See MADE IN CHINA, TRADE WARS

MAINSTREAM ECONOMICS

The predominant school of economic thinking taught worldwide in hundreds of universities by tens of thousands of professors, PhDs and ACADEMIC ECONOMISTS, none of whom were capable of predicting the worst post-WAR financial CRISIS any more than a month in advance.

MALINVESTMENTS

Literally, "bad INVESTMENTS". Malinvestments appear, and grow, when a CENTRAL BANK sets INTEREST RATES too low, thereby causing a CREDIT BUBBLE to blow up. The CREDIT BUBBLE then causes an appalling allocation of CREDIT. Quite simply, if you have to lend excessive amounts of MONEY as a BANKER, you simply have to lend it, even to obscure borrowers. (And your BOSS would sack you if you didn't.)

Starting in 2001, the malinvestment explosion became the driving force behind ECONOMIC GROWTH in DEVELOPED ECONOMIES, thus causing the SUBPRIME CRISIS in the USA and a similar CRISIS in some STATES of the EUROPEAN UNION. The bottom line: growth in GDP is not always good for the economy.
See AUSTRIAN SCHOOL, CREDIT CRUNCH

MARGINAL THEORY OF VALUE

If you are starving, a good sandwich has undeniable VALUE for you. If you are still hungry, you might eat another one, but its subjective VALUE for you would diminish. The VALUE of the third sandwich is likely to fall significantly for most people; some would still eat it, of course, especially if they didn't have to pay for it, but the marginal VALUE of the third sandwich drops to zero.

You are highly unlikely to eat the fourth sandwich, as its marginal value is probably going to be negative (at least for people with a normal stomach).

In contrast to the LABOUR THEORY OF VALUE, marginal theory assumes that the VALUE of things depends on your needs. Therefore, in the MARKET ECONOMY, VALUE is equal to the market price that you are willing to pay without coercion. This means that CAPITALISTS do not actually steal SURPLUS VALUE as claimed by MARX; there is therefore no need to send them to labour camps, and no need for food or clothes shortages, or indeed shortages of anything that money can buy. See LABOUR THEORY OF VALUE, MARKET ECONOMY

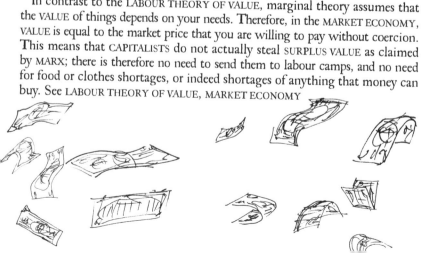

MARKET ECONOMY

An ECONOMIC system in which you can usually buy whatever you need and want, as long as you have MONEY. See CAPITALISM, COMMUNISM

MARRIAGE

A contract between three subjects: two PEOPLE, usually of the opposite SEX, and the STATE. See DIVORCE

Notable & Quotable
"MARRIAGE is a three ring circus: engagement ring, wedding ring, and suffering."
(Jessica Rowe)

MARX, *Karl*

The most famous and influential advocate of equality among PEOPLE (especially in terms of misery). Ironically enough, Marx is buried in LONDON, the most affluent city in the EUROPEAN UNION; most visitors to his grave are from CHINA, the nation that lost the most human lives trying to bring Marx's ideas into real life. His neighbour in Highgate Cemetery is Mr. Herbert Spencer, which is rather pleasing. Herbert Spencer was the ideological antithesis of Marx, being a CLASSICAL LIBERAL and often considered as a precursor to LIBERTARIANISM. See MARXISM, MARXIST ECONOMY, LABOUR THEORY OF VALUE, COMMUNISM, SOCIALISM

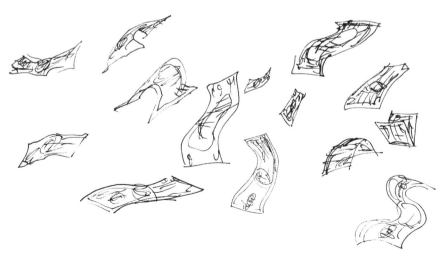

"*All the* EXPERIENCE *he had was in his own home, where his failure was catastrophic for his wife and family. Of his children some died of slow starvation and two committed suicide. Retaining and increasing all his* PROFESSIONAL *learning, he became more purely theoretical than even professors are allowed to be. Of the difficulties of organising human* SOCIETY *he knew practically nothing.*"

(C. Northcote PARKINSON: *"Left Luggage—From* MARX *to Wilson."* Penguin Books, 1967)

"*It is the* PEOPLE *who cannot manage their own affairs who feel most confident about ruling the world.*" (Herbert Spencer)

MARXISM

A doctrine which suggests that universal WEALTH and PROSPERITY is best achieved by universal EXPROPRIATION, and FREEDOM by all-embracing coercion.

MARXIST ECONOMY *(economic theory)*

Interestingly enough, Karl MARX and Friedrich Engels never seriously outlined what a properly run Marxist economy should look like. What they left behind was a lot of utopian ideas and the COMMUNIST Manifesto. The manifesto includes some more detailed points that are worthy of attention:

(1) The abolition of PROPERTY and the application of all land rents to public purposes. (Famine in CHINA in the 1960's and in Ukraine in the 1930's showed that this was not exactly the way to go.)

(2) A heavy progressive or graduated income TAX. (Done.)

(3) The abolition of all RIGHTS of inheritance. (Partly implemented by the inheritance TAX)

(4) The confiscation of the PROPERTY of all emigrants and rebels. (They wanted to confiscate all PROPERTY, in any case. All citizens with any PROPERTY were to be treated as enemies of the Marxist STATE.)

(5) The centralisation of CREDIT in the hands of the STATE by means of a national bank with STATE capital and an exclusive monopoly. (Almost done, considering the POWER of CENTRAL BANKS and GOVERNMENT regulators.)

(6) The centralisation of the means of communication and transport in the hands of the STATE. (Tried and failed.)

(7) The extension of factories and the instruments of production under the ownership of the STATE; the bringing into cultivation of waste-lands, and the improvement of the soil generally in accordance with a common plan. (Rather than direct ownership, which is associated with responsibility, the modern STATE prefers heavy-handed regulation, while responsibility remains in the hands of private owners.)

(8) The equal liability of all to labour. The establishment of industrial armies, especially for agriculture. (See POL POT)

(9) The combination of agriculture with manufacturing industries; the gradual abolition of the distinction between town and country by a more equitable distribution of the population across the country.
(See MAO ZEDONG)

(10) Free EDUCATION for all children in public schools. (As long as indoctrination can be considered EDUCATION.) The abolition of child labour in its present form and the combination of EDUCATION with industrial production. (More than accomplished with youth unemployment exceeding 50 per cent in SPAIN and GREECE.)

Different interpretations of the "real" MARXIST ECONOMY have been the source of debate, factional clashes, trials, executions and even military actions within COMMUNIST countries (see Alexander DUBČEK). To date, nobody knows for sure what a real Marxist economy actually is. See FASCISM, COMMUNISM

MASLOW'S HIERARCHY OF NEEDS

The hierarchy of essentials needed for human life. Originally proposed by Abraham Maslow in 1943. The list includes self-actualisation (creativity, morality, art), self-esteem (the DESIRE that your BOSS should at least know your surname), LOVE and belonging (if you can't have a dog or a cat then at least get married), safety (or an illusion of it; see JOB), physiological needs (food, water, air, SEX), and a Wi-Fi connection. The items are listed in order of increasing importance.

MCDONALD'S

One of the most successful and therefore most hated global CORPORATIONS. One anonymous author characterised McDonald's as a place where the customers are even more retarded than the workers. This may explain its extreme popularity worldwide. McDonald's is where social science graduates go to eat (and work). See GLOBALISATION, PHYSICS ENVY, SOCIAL SCIENCES

The Devil's Fashion Collection

MEAN/VARIANCE PORTFOLIO OPTIMISATION
A mathematical approach to PORTFOLIO management which aims to maximise the ratio of mean expected RETURNS to VOLATILITY. While being the subject of an indispensable chapter in every respectable textbook on PORTFOLIO management, optimisation is rarely used in practice. Why is this? If you follow the textbook recipe, the actual RETURNS achieved are usually very mean indeed.

MILLIONAIRE
In the good old days of the GOLD STANDARD, being a MILLIONAIRE meant being stupendously rich. Nowadays, anybody who owns a posh flat in a desirable location can proudly call himself a MILLIONAIRE. See BILLIONAIRE, INFLATION

Notable & Quotable
"Men will give away their last shirt to become MILLIONAIRES."
(A Yiddish proverb)

MINIMUM WAGE
A mechanism for pricing out the most vulnerable members of the JOB market and making them WELFARE-dependent.

MINSKY MOMENT
Hyman Minsky argued that lending goes through three distinct stages. He called these the Hedge, Speculative, and Ponzi stages (the latter after the financial fraudster, Charles Ponzi).

In the first stage, BANKS and DEBTORS are cautious. The DEBTOR is able to pay back the whole loan and the interest. As confidence rises, BANKS begin to grant larger loans. The DEBTOR can only afford to pay the interest. Finally, when the previous CRISIS becomes a distant memory, the economy reaches the final stage called Ponzi finance. BANKS make loans to DEBTORS who can afford to pay neither the interest nor the principal (see MALINVESTMENTs). This is supported by the belief that the price of EQUITIES and PROPERTY would rise without limit.

The "Minsky moment", a term coined by later economists, is the final stage when the whole house of cards collapses. When the BUBBLE bursts and the ASSET PRICES eventually plummet, BORROWERS and BANKS realise there is too much DEBT in the economy. PEOPLE rush to sell EQUITIES and PROPERTY causing a FINANCIAL PANIC and BANK RUNS.

This theory is strikingly similar to that of Ludwig von MISES and the AUSTRIAN SCHOOL. Yet Minsky was never a member of it. Why? See MINSKY, HYMAN in the section A PANOPTIC OF LUMINARIES AND THEIR INFAMOUS FINANCIAL FIASCOS.

MISES, *Ludwig von*

One of the few economists to have held the extreme view that correct and formal logic based on firm and obvious assumptions must necessarily lead to correct conclusions. Most modern mainstream economists consider this approach outdated and prefer DATA MINING instead. See AUSTRIAN SCHOOL, ROTHBARD

Ludwig von Mises

MISTRESS

1. A woman (other than the man's wife) who has a sexual relationship with a married man.
2. The primary consumer of LUXURY GOODS (the wife is the secondary).
3. A component of the political establishment in FRANCE.

MODEL

1. An attractive woman paid to advertise LUXURY GOODS.
2. A system of mathematical equations used by ACADEMIC ECONOMISTS to fool themselves; an over-sophisticated generator of random numbers.
See DSGE, CAPM, BLACK-SCHOLES MODEL, REAL BUSINESS CYCLE

Notable & Quotable
"All MODELS *are imperfect, but some are dangerous."*

Curious Fact: Male MODELS *underpaid*
Yes, there are also male MODELS. The Forbes magazine, which tracks the WEALTH of celebrities, POLITICIANS and other influential figures, releases its list of the world's highest-paid male models. According to the report, the 10 top-earning male models raked in a combined total of $8 million from September 2012 to September 2013—about one-tenth of the $83 million the 10 top-earning female models earned during that time.
Should male models whine about discrimination? No. That's just the way it is.

MONETARY POLICY

1. The most instrumental tool used by CENTRAL BANKS for mitigating fluctuations in the BUSINESS CYCLE.
2. A powerful way to debase CURRENCIES and kick-start economic RECESSIONS.
3. One of the ways central authorities pretend to solve CRISES.
4. The primary cause of INFLATION and the gradual erosion of the purchasing power of your SAVINGS.
See REAL BUSINESS CYCLE, EXPANSIVE MONETARY POLICY, RESTRICTIVE MONETARY POLICY

Curious Question: Is monetary policy effective?
Is MONETARY POLICY really all that effective? Opinions vary.
   In the words of pseudo NOBEL ECONOMICS PRIZE laureate, Professor Edward Prescott: *"It is an established scientific fact that* MONETARY POLICY *has had virtually no effect on output and employment in the U.S. since the formation of the* FED.*"*
   Most other economics professors, not to mention CENTRAL BANKERS, would disagree. MAINSTREAM opinion considers MONETARY POLICY essential.
   Then there is the AUSTRIAN SCHOOL of economics, which argues that CENTRAL BANK MONETARY POLICY aggravates the BUSINESS CYCLE, creating MALINVESTMENTS in the economy.
   Decide for yourself where the truth lies.

The fact of the matter is that since the inception of modern MONETARY POLICY, which can be dated to 1973 (the final demise of the GOLD STANDARD), the UNEMPLOYMENT rate has risen in most developed countries, while the rate of ECONOMIC GROWTH has fallen. Just a coincidence? A Mephistophelian question indeed.

MONEY
The universal means of exchange, which can buy most items on MASLOW'S HIERARCHY OF NEEDS in all systems, in CAPITALISM as well as in SOCIALISM; one of the main things that makes humans different from animals.

Notable & Quotable
"MONEY: *A blessing that is of no advantage to us excepting when we part with it. An evidence of culture and a passport to polite* SOCIETY. *Supportable* PROPERTY." (Ambrose Bierce, The Devil's Dictionary)

MONEY, (fiat)
Fiat money is a modern form of MONEY which has no material substance and as such may be freely and easily debased by CENTRAL BANKS. See CURRENCY, CURRENCY DEBASEMENT, INFLATION, MONETARY POLICY, GOLD STANDARD

MONEY SUPPLY
The total sum of MONEY that circulates in the economy, from banknotes to current accounts to deposit and SAVINGS accounts. Growth in the MONEY supply causes monetary INFLATION, which is the key engine behind long-term price increases in PROPERTY, EQUITIES and COMMODITIES.

Curious Fact: Housing too expensive? Blame the money suply!
The total sum of MONEY in cash and BANK accounts in GREAT BRITAIN grew at an average rate of 7 per cent per annum from December 1993 to December 2013, which means in that period the MONEY SUPPLY almost quadrupled. This is why the average price of a family house in Britain went up 3.3 times, according to the Nationwide Building Society. (Now that's INFLATION! And is very different from the CONSUMER PRICE INDEX.)

Looking back, we learn that 85 per cent of new houses sold for less than £750 in the 1930's. (Note it was 750 pounds, not thousands of pounds.) Terraced houses in the Greater LONDON area could be bought for £395 in the mid-1930's, when AVERAGE EARNINGS were about £165 per year.

Over the next eighty years, a similar house might fetch a thousand times its original PRICE (or more). This translates as a 9 per cent annual average price increase, not including the rental YIELD. It's a devilish idea that the same house might cost as much as £395 million in another eighty years. And why not? The sky's the limit in an economy based on a fiat CURRENCY.

MONTE CARLO
1. The famous casino where you can lose a great deal of MONEY in the blink of an eye.
2. A mathematical method of simulating complex processes in finance used by QUANTS, which may end up losing a great deal of OTHER PEOPLE'S MONEY.

MORAL HAZARD
The chance to play with OTHER PEOPLE'S MONEY with zero risk of being punished if things go pear-shaped.
See BANKS, INVESTMENT BANKS, GOVERNMENT, MANAGERS

MORTGAGE
Get your own home for the devilish PRICE of a DEBT burden that you will have to carry for decades; a form of voluntary slavery that PEOPLE sign up to in their millions. See DEBTOR

MUST *(verb)*
The favourite word of the political left. See DICTATORSHIP, SOCIALISM

Money supply growth

NATIONAL SOCIALISM

A special variety of SOCIALISM where the oppressed and the benefactor classes are, respectively, defined by the ethnic or racial key. Most popular in GERMANY from 1933 and throughout WORLD WAR II until, allegedly, 1945.
See FASCISM, REAL SOCIALISM, SOCIALISM

Devil's Question: Leftist Nazism?

Why is NATIONAL SOCIALISM considered to be a political movement of the far right when the Nazis themselves called it "SOCIALISM"? The answer is pretty simple. The allied POWERS were mostly dominated by the political left in 1945, from NEW DEAL America to LABOUR-led Britain to STALIN's RUSSIA. As history is written by the victors, NATIONAL SOCIALISM has been labelled "far right", to the permanent irritation of CLASSICAL LIBERALS and LIBERTARIANS. It was, of course, far right of STALIN.

Yet NATIONAL SOCIALISM was decidedly leftist in many respects. Hitler introduced four-year economic plans, where most COMMUNIST countries used five-year plans. CONFISCATION, PRICE controls, GOVERNMENT monopoly on foreign trade, GOVERNMENT monopoly on education, PROGRESSIVE TAXATION: all of this was common both for NATIONAL SOCIALISM and MARXISM-inspired REAL SOCIALISM. All kinds of SOCIALISM have been collectivist in nature; see COMMON GOOD.

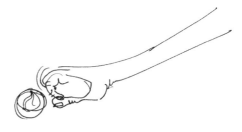

Devil's Question: FASCISM *or* NATIONAL SOCIALISM?

Communists and SOCIALISTS have never been happy that Hitler chose the brand name "NATIONAL SOCIALISM" for his movement. As early as December 1933, the Comintern (an international communist organization based in Moscow and governed by STALIN) defined "FASCISM" as follows:

"FASCISM is the undisguised terrorist DICTATORSHIP of the most reactionary, most chauvinistic, and most imperialistic elements of finance CAPITAL."

Chauvinistic, yes; imperialistic, certainly; but finance CAPITAL behind a DICTATORSHIP? The truth was that many financial CAPITALISTS were happy to leave GERMANY with their bare lives and left most of their WEALTH behind. Those who remained were progressively TAXED and totally subjugated to the NATIONAL SOCIALIST German Workers' Party, aka the Nationalsozialistische Deutsche Arbeiterpartei or NSDAP for short.

There is not a single piece of evidence that the Nazis were ruled by BANKERS as the Comintern definition would suggest. On the contrary, when Hjalmar Schacht, the Nazi economy minister and a BANKER himself, tried to oppose Hitler's armament plans on the grounds of budget stability, he was dismissed and later sent to a concentration camp.

Still, the above-mentioned unfriendly definition was no obstacle to STALIN's forming a pact with Hitler; the pact only ended with the German invasion of the Soviet Union in June 1941.

Notable & Quotable

"I am a SOCIALIST, because it appears incomprehensible to me to maintain a machine with care and concern, but to leave the noblest representative of work, the man himself, in deprivation." (Adolf Hitler)

Diabolical Fact: Ordinary Germans benefited from national socialism

"The Nazi leaders were constantly handing out benefits to ordinary Germans, keeping them remarkably well fed and well supplied. At the same time, those who possessed the financial know-how compensated as best they could for the state's generosity. They kept increasing taxes on GERMANY's *wealthy, not because they thought that made the most sense, but because it was the only option for raising* TAXES *within the country."*

(Götz Aly, German historian and author of *"Hitler's Beneficiaries: Plunder, Racial War and the Nazi Welfare State"*)

NATIONALISATION

1. The EXPROPRIATION of private CAPITAL, carried out extensively in REAL SOCIALISM and in post-war Britain, followed by PRIVATISATION when socialist countries went bust and Margaret THATCHER became Prime Minister.

2. Code name for the BANK BAILOUT after the financial CRISIS in Britain and continental EUROPE which started in 2007.

NEOLIBERALISM

1. Allegedly the world's most powerful ECONOMIC doctrine. However, neoliberalism has precisely no followers, supporters or apologists. As an economic school of thought, it simply doesn't exist. Nor does it as a political movement.

2. The universal culprit for all of the POVERTY and hardship in the world.

3. A code name for the WASHINGTON CONSENSUS used, however, solely by its opponents.

NET PRESENT VALUE
The sum of the VALUE of castles in the air, discounted by GREED and fear.

$$\frac{z_1}{1+r} + \frac{z_2}{(1+r)^2}$$

NEW DEAL

A complex of economic policies pursued by US president Franklin Delano ROOSEVELT as a response to the GREAT DEPRESSION of the 1930's. The name refers to the new distribution of playing cards in the economy which meant the GOVERNMENT became the single most important player and BANKER all in one.

Curious Question: NEW DEAL—*success or failure?*

Was the NEW DEAL a success or a failure? Opinions differ. The traditional view holds that ROOSEVELT saved the US economy from total and final destruction. It is true that BANKS recovered during ROOSEVELT's term and that the NEW DEAL regulation of WALL STREET worked well for decades after its introduction.

On the other hand, the NEW DEAL failed to cope with UNEMPLOYMENT. UNEMPLOYMENT went as high as 20 per cent in June 1938, five years after the NEW DEAL had been launched. German propaganda of the time derided America with much SCHADENFREUDE for that reason.

UNEMPLOYMENT only fell below the 10 per cent mark in February 1941. In terms of the LABOUR market, the NEW DEAL was indeed a huge failure.

NEW NORMAL

A euphemism for the stagnation of ECONOMIC GROWTH in over-DEVELOPED countries. See DEGROWTH, ZERO-GROWTH

NOBEL PRIZE FOR ECONOMIC SCIENCES

1. Officially known as *"The Sveriges Riksbank Prize in Economic Sciences in Memory of Alfred Nobel"*. Awarded to only the very best ACADEMIC ECONOMISTS for their lasting intellectual contribution to the profession.
2. The pseudo NOBEL PRIZE which Alfred NOBEL did not mention in his will; created in 1969 to give the illusion that ECONOMICS is indeed a science.

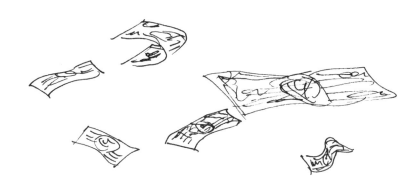

OCCUPY WALL STREET

Demonstration by rich kids against the system that made their parents rich.

Curious Fact: Well-off protesters

A third of protesters in the Occupy WALL STREET movement in New York lived in households earning more than $100,000 and more than two thirds were employed PROFESSIONALS, according to a study from CUNY's Joseph A. Murphy Institute for Worker EDUCATION and LABOR Studies.

The study also showed that the movement was mostly organized by experienced political operatives and nearly all of those involved – 76 per cent – were college educated. Of those, half had graduate DEGREES and among those with bachelor's DEGREES, 28 per cent had attended elite universities.

"It's a pretty affluent demographic and highly educated," said Professor Ruth Milkman, one of the study's authors. *"Many were the children of the elite, if you will."* New York Post, 29 January 2013

OFF-BALANCE ITEMS

ACCOUNTING items which too often tend to move onto a BALANCE SHEET where they eat profits. See PROFIT (LOSS) STATEMENT

OLIGARCHY

GOVERNMENT by a small group of people; not necessarily OLIGARCHS, but often BUREAUCRATS pretending to rule in the name of the COMMON GOOD.

OLIGARCHS

Extremely rich PEOPLE, usually in EMERGING MARKETS like RUSSIA; their primary activity is to extract wealth from their home countries and siphon it off to the LONDON PROPERTY market and HARROD'S. See LUXURY GOODS

OPTIMUM CURRENCY AREA

A territory consisting of one or more countries or regions which share similar economic characteristics; it is thus reasonable for them to use a single CURRENCY. Disregarding this rule may cause difficulties for weaker countries or regions which cannot bear the burden of too hard a CURRENCY. Ignoring the optimum CURRENCY area theory also brings trouble to the stronger countries or regions as they must subsidise the weaker ones. See EURO, EUROZONE

OTHER PEOPLE'S MONEY

1. An inexhaustible and renewable resource freely and readily available for the GOVERNMENT to use.

2. BANKERS' toy of choice

3. Your MONEY

OUT OF THIN AIR

A modern method of producing MONEY. A few clicks on a computer keyboard and a CENTRAL BANK has unlimited billions of the CURRENCY it is responsible for: dollars, pounds, yen, EUROS, Thai baht, Swedish krona, Czech koruna, you name it. No GOLD backing is necessary, no GOVERNMENT or PARLIAMENT approval required. In an age of independent CENTRAL BANKS, a handful of CENTRAL BANKERS can create MONEY at will. They don't even need the proverbial printing press. See INFLATION

OUTSOURCING

The process of closing factories in DEVELOPED MARKETS and relocating them to EMERGING MARKETS. Cost cutting usually works perfectly well until the point at which most of the fired workers in the DEVELOPED MARKETS have no more MONEY to spend. The rest, however, are more than happy to buy inferior products from CHINA as there's no other choice. The office for statistics is enthusiastic, too, as the inferior products from CHINA help to keep INFLATION down. See MADE IN CHINA

OVERHEATED ECONOMY

1. An economy producing more than its long-term potential, due especially to the ample growth of MALINVESTMENTS during the Ponzi stage and before the MINSKY MOMENT occurs.

2. The overtaxed and BUREAUCRACY-burdened EUROZONE economy galloping along at 0.3 per cent.

PARKINSON, *Cyril Northcote*
A British naval historian and prolific writer (1909–1993). He was also one of the greatest economic thinkers of the 20th century, although his ground-breaking work in the field has mistakenly been thought of as merely a collection of satirical essays.

Some of his observations entered the public domain, such as the following:

a) Expenditure rises to meet income.

b) When an organisational entity expands beyond 21 members, the real POWER will be in some smaller body.

c) Expansion means complexity and complexity decay.

d) Time spent on any item of the agenda will be in inverse proportion to the sums involved.

e) Make the PEOPLE SOVEREIGN and the poor will use the machinery of GOVERNMENT to dispossess the rich.

f) Perfection in planning is achieved only by institutions on the point of collapse.

American economist William Niskanen (1933-2011) elaborated many of PARKINSON's ideas into academic hypotheses and articles about BUREAUCRACY and the pitfalls of collective decision making. Sadly, Niskanen died before the NOBEL PRIZE committee had a chance to award him a well-deserved prize. See GROUPTHINK, EUROPEAN UNION

PARLIAMENT
The place where the interests of pressure groups and LOBBYISTS are moulded into laws. See PEOPLE, POLITICIANS

PAY-AS-YOU-GO SOCIAL SECURITY SCHEME (PAYG)
A system whereby provision for the elderly is paid from SOCIAL SECURITY contributions by active workers. Originally conceived as an ingenious system completely immune to STOCK MARKET fluctuations and largely independent of the BUSINESS CYCLE. In latter decades, however, it has turned out that the PAYG scheme has two shortcomings. First, the social security TAX burden makes LABOUR more expensive, resulting in chronically lower demand for LABOUR and thus to chronic UNEMPLOYMENT. Secondly, such a false sense of SECURITY has partly replaced the most traditional way of securing an income in old age: children.

Curious Fact: SOCIAL SECURITY *destroys family formation and fertility*
"*There is growing concern about a decline in the total fertility rate worldwide, but nowhere is the concern greater than in* DEVELOPED COUNTRIES, *some of which already face the prospect of population decline as well. (...) Our paper indicates that it is partly influenced by the scale of the defined-benefits pay-as-you-go (PAYG)* SOCIAL SECURITY *systems operating in most countries. (...) We show analytically that social security tax and benefit rates generate incentives for individuals to reduce not just the fertility rate within families, but also the incentive to form families. (...) Our results show that the impact of* SOCIAL SECURITY *on net marriage and total fertility rates has been non-trivial.*"
(Isaac Ehrlich and Jinyoung Kim: *Has social security influenced family formation and fertility in OECD countries?* An economic and econometric analysis. NBER Working Paper, 2007)

Devil's Question: When will DEMOCRACIES *turn into gerontocracies?*
"*An impending demographic* CRISIS *in* GERMANY *calls for fundamental reforms of the pension system. In a democracy, however, reforms require the support of the majority of the electorate. To determine whether the majority is in favour of reforms of the pension system, we calculate for each year the 'indifference age' as the age of the cohort that is not affected by the reform and the 'median age' as the age of the politically decisive cohort. Until 2016, a reform can be democratically enforced. After 2016,* GERMANY *will be a gerontocracy.*"
(Hans-Werner Sinn and Silke Uebelmesser: *Pensions and the path to gerontocracy in* GERMANY. European Journal of Political Economy, 2002)

PEER-TO-PEER LENDING
Fat cat free lending and borrowing.

PEOPLE, *The*
The only SOVEREIGN source of POWER in democratic countries, after LOBBYISTS and INTEREST GROUPS. See PARLIAMENT

PERMABEARS
1. Wise sages who keep giving us warnings before a total and irreparable market meltdown.
2. Gurus who always bet on the WORST-CASE SCENARIO, regardless of facts and figures, just to look superficially prudent.

PHD *(in economics)*
A common form of MALINVESTMENT of intellectual resources. See EDUCATION

Diabolical Fact: Want to get rich? Drop out of college!
According to the 2011 Forbes 400 list of BILLIONAIRES, 63 earned only a high school diploma. Most of them earned rather than inherited their WEALTH. Then there are the BILLIONAIRE college dropouts, whose average net worth was $9.4 billion. By contrast, the average net worth of BILLIONAIRES with PhDs was $3.2 billion. There were also more college dropouts than PhDs on the 2011 Forbes 400 BILLIONAIRE list: 63 compared to 21.

Disclaimer: neither the author nor the publisher of this book bears any responsibility whatsoever for readers' decisions concerning their higher EDUCATION and career choices. In short, don't drop out of school unless you're another Bill Gates or Steve Jobs.

PHYSICS ENVY

An unhappy feeling common among economists when they compare their own discipline to the natural sciences.

Notable & Quotable

"Economists want to be taken seriously and so have to clutter up their work with complex equations no one reads or cares about so that no one will mistake them for sociologists." (Anonymous commenter at marginalrevolution.com)

POLITICIAN

1. A person who you, the TAXPAYER, hire to take care of public affairs. See PEOPLE

2. A person who thinks they are your BOSS. See PUBLIC SERVANT

Notable & Quotable

"The difference between PROSTITUTES and POLITICIANS? The former sells what is rightfully hers. The latter peddles stolen goods."
(Rothbardian, @Sebastian_JKT)
"Difference between a voter and his congressman: the voter has to earn what he spends." (Philip Schuyler, @FiveRights)

POLITICS

The process of constantly searching for a compromise in affairs concerning POWER and MONEY. The compromise means that TAXPAYERS believe they pay too much; poorer voters feel they receive insufficient entitlements; POLITICIANS are convinced they need yet more POWER and MONEY to implement all their wonderful projects in the name of the COMMON GOOD; and PUBLIC DEBT is growing. See ELECTIONS, DEMOCRACY, POLITIK

POLITICAL CYCLE

In democratic countries, GOVERNMENTS generally change every two to four years (depending on the degree of political stability). The incumbent GOVERNMENT thinks it can buy votes by increasing spending in the run-up to the ELECTION. The new GOVERNMENT feels it must not cut that spending. And so the cycle goes on and on for decades until GOVERNMENT DEBT reaches seriously nasty levels. See BANKRUPTCY, DEFAULT

POLITIK

1. Politics done the German way.
2. Politik is the continuation of war by other means.

PONZI SCHEME

A financial redistribution scheme which guarantees high RETURNS for its participants, assuming there is an infinite number of new entrants. See MINSKY MOMENT, PAY-AS-YOU-GO

PORTFOLIO
A set of randomly chosen low-yielding bonds, risky EQUITIES and overpriced, fee-burdened INVESTMENT FUNDS, mostly purchased at a high PRICE and eventually sold by CLIENTS in utter panic at a ridiculously low PRICE. See INVESTMENT DECISION CYCLE

POTENTIAL ECONOMIC GROWTH
A number which is close to zero when the impact of growing DEBT—both GOVERNMENT and private—is subtracted. See GDP, ECONOMIC GROWTH

POVERTY
A necessary condition for the success of political parties that declare their intention to eradicate it. POLITICIANS who claim to defend the poor and UNEMPLOYED therefore need there to be quite a lot of poverty and UNEMPLOYMENT.

POWER
The ultimate VALUE revered by most politicians.

PRICE/EARNINGS RATIO, P/E
A measure of equity valuation, which fails most miserably when you most need it. See SHILLER'S P/E

Curious Fact: Ditch the P/E
The P/E ratio could not even be defined in February and March 2009 for some important STOCK MARKETS and indices, including the S&P 500 and the Dow Jones. This was when EQUITIES were the cheapest they had been in any decade since the late 1970's. The P/E epically failed to signal this unique opportunity!

PRINCIPAL-AGENT PROBLEM
I am the owner of an estate. I appoint you as the manager of the estate and leave you alone for a year or more. Can you really resist the excruciating temptation to add something to your salary?

PRIVATISATION
1. The process of transforming PUBLIC OWNERSHIP into private ownership.
2. A unique chance to perform ASSET STRIPPING or TUNNELLING on a large scale.

PROFIT (LOSS) STATEMENT

The reason why accountants and AUDITORS write negative numbers in parentheses.

PROFESSIONAL

A person who knows either what to do or how to do it; only in very rare cases do they know both.

PROGRESSIVE TAXATION

1. The system of income TAX RATES which rise with the TAXPAYER's income.
2. A way to punish the most efficient economic subjects.
3. A wartime measure to extract maximum MONEY from TAXPAYERS, which, unlike food rationing or retail PRICE regulation, has survived to the present day.
See FLAT TAX, NATIONAL SOCIALISM

Curiuos Fact: High TAX *rates do not bring about high* PROSPERITY
An array of poor DEVELOPING COUNTRIES has been experimenting with steeply progressive TAX rates. Sudan, for instance, taxed top earners, both individuals and CORPORATIONS, by the marginal rate of 60 per cent. Everybody knows it has been a tremendous success.

In 2013, the Republic of CHAD was the country with the steepest progressive individual income TAX rate, reaching 60 per cent of income above the annual income equivalent of £7,600. Congratulations N'Djamena.

PROPERTY
1. Buildings or land. Also called real estate in order to emphasise the fact of its real existence as opposed to some securities and virtual currencies. Real estate PRICES may sometimes, however, reach surreal VALUES.
2. The world's favourite speculative market, where large sums of borrowed MONEY are invested; excess investment in PROPERTY has caused nine of the eleven post-war RECESSIONS in the USA.
See MALINVESTMENT, LONDON, DETROIT

PROSPERITY
The warm feeling that you have a JOB, a home, a car and a full fridge, marred only by the fact that your JOB is insecure, your home is MORTGAGED, you neighbour has a better car, and your cholesterol level is sky high.

The Devil's Fashion Collection

PROSTITUTION

A special type of MARRIAGE, contracted for a very short period, sometimes measured in minutes, depending on the man's experience and physical condition. Unlike short term INVESTMENTS, prostitution is significantly risky. DIVERSIFICATION is no help, either.

Curious Fact: MARRIAGE *for one night*

In certain cultures which generally ban adultery, PROSTITUTION has indeed had the legal form of a short term MARRIAGE contract. Temporary MARRIAGES have been taking place in the southern part of INDIA, where rich foreigners have been exploiting poverty-stricken Muslim families.

Rich men, mostly from the MIDDLE EAST and Africa, marry young Muslim girls under the garb of Islam and pay off their families. As PROSTITUTION is forbidden under Islam, these temporary MARRIAGES (nikah al-mut'ah) provide a loophole. As a rule, the parents are poor and force their daughters into the temporary MARRIAGES under the guise of religion in order to earn MONEY. (There are legal disputes as to whether Muhammad banned it or not, but many pious Muslims just aren't that bothered.)

The duration of the MARRIAGE is decided beforehand, and the DIVORCE proceedings are started at the time of MARRIAGE in order to hasten the process. Sometimes the MARRIAGE is for a month, sometimes for a week, and at times just for one night. You can probably guess how the "bride" feels after such a wedding night.

Curious Fact: Fourth of July, an unlikely holiday
Economists Steven Levitt and Sudhir Alladi Venkatesh wrote a paper called
'An Empirical Analysis of Street-Level Prostitution'. This noteworthy
piece of research focuses on the economic aspects of the world's second
oldest profession (see SEX WORKERS), including those DETAILS that may not
bear thinking about.

The researchers found, for example, that *"in response to a predictable demand
shock associated with the 4th of July holiday, the supply of* PROSTITUTES
*proves to be fairly elastic. Total quantity increases by 60 per cent that week
through a combination of increased work by existing* PROSTITUTES*, short-term
substitution into* PROSTITUTION *by women who do not trade* SEX *for* MONEY
most of the year, and the temporary inflow of outside PROSTITUTES*. The* PRICE
increase associated with the 4th of July demand shock is 30 per cent."

Now I will always remember Levitt and Venkatesh every 4th of July.

PROTECTIONISM

The old practice of shielding a country's domestic industries from foreign COMPETITION by creating obstacles to imports. Protectionism creates trade barriers and trade barriers are one of the main causes of WARS. See WORLD WAR I

Notable & Quotable

A former British prime minister, Lord Salisbury, admonished the French ambassador in the late 19th century as follows: *"If you were not such persistent protectionists, you would not find us so keen to annex territories!"*

Curious Fact: PROTECTIONISM *caused the Great War*

"By 1913, GERMANY *had 60,000 university students to Britain's 9,000, and 3,000 engineering students to Britain's 350. German industries were not only out-producing Britain, they were producing superior products."*
(D. J. Goodspeed, *The German* WARS. New York, Bonanza Books, 1985)

"...These 'two hostile POWER *groupings' were the old imperial centers of* CAPITAL, *Britain and her allies, and the emerging imperial centers of* CAPITAL, GERMANY *and her allies. Restrictive trade practices were strangling potentially* WEALTHY *countries and 'everyone knew it would start but no one knew how or when ... until Archduke Ferdinand was shot.'"*
(Lawrence Malkin, *The National* DEBT. New York, Henry Holt and Co., 1988)

PUBLIC DEBT

1. A financial obligation which will improve our chances of winning another ELECTION, and will be paid for by the children of our political opponents sometime in the future (POLITICIAN's view).
2. A financial obligation which will improve the life of leisure of the lazy underclass today, but will be paid for by our children (TAXPAYER's view).

PUBLIC EXPENDITURE

Spending which is paid for by so many TAXPAYERS and planned by so few GOVERNMENT POLITICIANS. See PUBLIC DEBT, MORAL HAZARD

PUBLIC OWNERSHIP

See PRINCIPAL-AGENT PROBLEM and magnify it by a factor of between 1,000 and 1,000,000.

PUBLIC SERVANT
A GOVERNMENT official who believes the public is their servant.
See BUREAUCRAT, INTEREST GROUPS

PUBLIC SERVICES
A method of creating artificial JOBS to employ more PUBLIC SERVANTS.

PUBLICLY TRADED COMPANY

A company which is at least partly owned by a large number of distributed shareholders who can trade its shares on the STOCK EXCHANGE. Some companies are entirely owned by distributed shareholders, which in fact means they are owned by no-one. See PRINCIPAL-AGENT PROBLEM

QUANTITATIVE EASING

1. An unconventional way of conducting expansionary MONETARY POLICY used by CENTRAL BANKS to stimulate ECONOMIC GROWTH when standard policies fail. In short, the CENTRAL BANK wants you to spend your MONEY so tries to convince you that your MONEY will lose its VALUE faster than you would have thought. This is supposed to make you spend like mad. Believe it or not, the CENTRAL BANK thinks that by depleting your SAVINGS it will improve the economy.

2. Inflating the BUBBLE by innovative means; however, quantitative easing makes it more difficult to buy, e.g., a home due to monetary INFLATION.

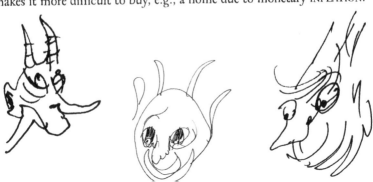

QUANTITY THEORY OF MONEY
In theory, pumping MONEY into an economy should boost ECONOMIC GROWTH or INFLATION, or both, thereby making you richer. In fact, it usually boosts INFLATION, thereby making you poorer. See QUANTITATIVE EASING

QUANTS
Second-rate nuclear physicists and rocket scientists who aren't good enough to make it to CERN, CalTech, NASA or JPL, but still sufficiently smart to impress BANK BOSSES, so hired as quantitative analysts to produce supposedly ingenious algorithms in order to outsmart the market. Not smart enough to admit their own futility, however.
See EFFICIENT MARKETS, INVESTMENT BANK, TRADERS

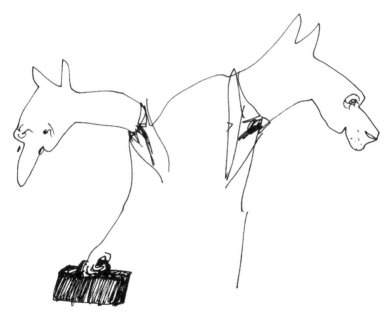

QUEEN'S QUESTION
During her visit to the LONDON School of ECONOMICS in November 2008, Queen Elizabeth II asked: *"Why did nobody notice it?"*

She was, of course, referring to the CRISIS in the international financial markets. The Queen's personal fortune was estimated to have fallen by 25 per cent (from a VALUE of £320 million) during the early stages of the CRISIS.

Professor Luis Garicano, director of research at the LSE's management department, told the Queen: *"At every stage, someone was relying on somebody else and everyone thought they were doing the right thing."*

Although the professors from the LSE wrote a lengthy letter soon after the Queen's visit, Garicano's reply was perhaps the best answer. It illustrated the principle of GROUPTHINK and HERD BEHAVIOUR, which were the main reasons for the CRISIS.

RADICAL
A person who supports a REVOLUTION hoping they will be better off with a change of despot.

RATING
An assessment of the CREDIT quality and SOLVENCY of CORPORATIONS and GOVERNMENTS, which usually lags behind the publicly known facts.

REAL BUSINESS CYCLE
An academic theory which explains fluctuations in ECONOMIC GROWTH. The real business cycle (RBC) theory assumes that MONETARY POLICY does not have an effect on GDP. Since 1982, when RBC theory appeared, a number of PEOPLE have added "frictions" to the model so that MONETARY POLICY does have real effects. (Does it work? For producing academic papers, yes it does. But don't expect practical results.)

REAL ECONOMY

A derogatory term for outdated stuff like factories, manufacturing, construction and other mostly obsolete industries which produce dull and boring tangible things like food, clothes, cars, furniture, appliances and so on. Modern ECONOMICS pays little attention to it. If the economy doesn't fit the MODEL, ignore the economy. See REAL BUSINESS CYCLE, DSGE

REAL SOCIALISM

A version of SOCIALISM specific to the former Soviet bloc. Marxist theorists assumed that CAPITALISM would be replaced by real socialism after a revolution; nevertheless, real SOCIALISM should itself be replaced by COMMUNISM in a gradual way.

Apparently, the wish list of Marxists did not include REVOLUTION against themselves. Real SOCIALISM was therefore based on a totalitarian STATE and full GOVERNMENT ownership of CAPITAL; this eventually led to obsolescence, loss of COMPETITIVENESS, and terminal decay of the system in the late 1980's. See COMMUNISM, FASCISM

RECESSION

1. An intermission in ECONOMIC GROWTH lasting at least two consecutive quarters, which usually occurs once every couple of years. RECESSIONS are necessary for improving efficiency, removing possible BUBBLES and restoring soundness and reason to the economy.
2. A good excuse to sack PEOPLE and outsource JOBS to CHINA.
3. A modern euphemism for CRISIS.
4. The normal modus operandi of most EU economies.

RESTRICTIVE FISCAL POLICY
Usually following periods of expansive MONETARY POLICY, restrictive fiscal policy (AUSTERITY by any other name) attempts to tame the growth of GOVERNMENT DEBT by hiking TAX rates above the pain threshold. It usually causes a RECESSION, possibly a CRISIS, and ever greater GOVERNMENT DEBT.

RESTRICTIVE MONETARY POLICY
The CENTRAL BANK increases INTEREST RATES, which in turn causes a decline in CREDIT creation; this will usually tame INFLATION, but may also cause a RECESSION or even a BANKING CRISIS and a CREDIT CRUNCH.

RETURNS
Expected returns: Pure hope – or hopium (the term preferred by PERMABEARS).

Historical returns: No guarantee of future performance (or indeed of anything).

Real returns: What remains after INFLATION is accounted for.

Realised returns: What the GOVERNMENT always wants to TAX.

Realised losses: What the GOVERNMENT will never compensate you for, unless you're a BANK. See AVERAGE RETURNS

REVOLUTION
The ultimate act of popular despair, which usually ends with the replacement of the old despot with a new despot, who is usually worse than the old one.
See CONSERVATIVE, RADICAL, REAL SOCIALISM

RIGHTS *(basic, civil, human)*
Originally, basic civil rights included only those mentioned in the United States Declaration of Independence published in **1776**:

"We hold these truths to be self-evident, that all men are created equal, that they are endowed by their Creator with certain unalienable Rights, and that among these are Life, Liberty and the pursuit of Happiness."

Over the centuries, the number of rights has grown to include all kinds of WELFARE and PUBLIC SERVICES, from SOCIAL INSURANCE to free Wi-Fi hotspots. Obviously, social rights have become increasingly costly, and this creates a heavy TAX burden.

See SOCIALISTS, HANDOUTS, ENTITLEMENTS, INTEREST GROUPS

Notable & Quotable
"The New Zealand constitution grants the fewest RIGHTS, namely zero, while the Bolivian constitution grants the most rights, at 88. VENEZUELA offers almost as many rights in its CONSTITUTION as Bolivia. Nevertheless, I think I would feel more secure in my RIGHTS living in New Zealand than Bolivia or VENEZUELA. A CONSTITUTION with a long list of RIGHTS is a bit like a prenup with a long list of RIGHTS: looks good on parchment but parchment does not a MARRIAGE or a CONSTITUTION make." (Alex Tabarrok)

RISK
1. The possibility that the expected RETURN on an INVESTMENT may in fact be negative.
2. A theoretical concept which is especially hard to explain to amateur INVESTORS during BULL MARKETS, but becomes very easy to grasp during BEAR MARKETS.

See INTEREST RATE RISK

RISK-FREE BONDS
BONDS of DEVELOPED countries thought to be very safe. INVESTORS normally believe that RISK-free BONDS in your PORTFOLIO will mature earlier than the indebted countries will DEFAULT.

See HIGH-YIELD BONDS, INTEREST RATE RISK

ROTHBARD, MURRAY

The economist who claimed that a state-run monopoly on MONEY and MONETARY POLICY would inevitably lead to INFLATION. The hypothesis proved correct, yet Rothbard is hardly mentioned in MAINSTREAM ECONOMIC courses and textbooks. See AUSTRIAN SCHOOL, MISES

Murray Rothbard

Notable & Quotable
"INFLATION *of the* MONEY SUPPLY *destroys the* VALUE *of the dollar or pound, drives up* PRICES, *cripples economic calculation, and hobbles and seriously damages the workings of the* MARKET ECONOMY.*" (Murray Rothbard)

SAVINGS

1. Financial reserves for your future.

2. Something undesirable that, according to CENTRAL BANKS and GOVERNMENTS, undermines ECONOMIC GROWTH. If you squander your savings, however, you help to increase GDP!

3. Your MONEY deposited at a bank where it can easily be debauched by INFLATION, taxed, and possibly also confiscated if the GOVERNMENT decides so to do.

SCHADENFREUDE

The pleasure derived from another person's misfortune. Imported into English from German, like blitz, flak, kitsch, weltschmerz, angst, realpolitik and hamburger.

SECURITIES
Paper INVESTMENTS which can sometimes become rather insecure.
See EQUITIES, BONDS, RISK

SELF-EMPLOYED *(worker)*
Somebody who decides they don't need a BOSS, only to find that it is the customer who is the real master. Warning: self-employment can become serf-employment with surprising ease.

SEX

1. The way humans reproduce (unlike ACADEMIC ECONOMISTS who reproduce asexually, by graduation).

2. A popular diversion which is usually free and does not, therefore, improve GDP; SEX is not even taxable. When paid for, SEX becomes an element of the shadow economy. (If regularly paid to a single partner, see MARRIAGE.)

3. The ultimate VALUE for most males, whether human or animal, second only to Wi-Fi.

SEX WORKER

The second oldest human profession, preceded only by hunter-gathering. See PROSTITUTION

SHADOW ECONOMY
Includes those economic activities (and the income derived from them) that circumvent or avoid GOVERNMENT regulation or taxation, for example, MONEY laundering, illicit drugs, illegal gambling, SEX for MONEY (not including SEX in MARRIAGE, however dearly it's paid for), untaxed work like babysitting, and other such deadly sins.

SHILLER'S P/E
A version of P/E modified by pseudo NOBEL PRIZE laureate Robert Shiller. Shiller's P/E assumes that earnings figures up to ten years old can contain some forecasting POWER. Sorry, they can't.

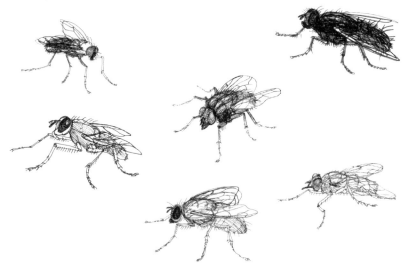

SICK MAN OF EUROPE
The sick man of EUROPE is a label used for the continent's weak economies. Given the wide variety of bad economic policies practised from Lisbon to Moscow and Brussels to Istanbul, there have always been some sick men of EUROPE. Originally used by the Russian tsar in the 1850's to denote Turkey, and later for a number of other countries, including RUSSIA herself. More recently, used for GREAT BRITAIN in the 1970's, GERMANY in the 1990's, and FRANCE, ITALY, PORTUGAL and GREECE during the European financial CRISIS. See TIGER ECONOMY

"Today, the sick man of EUROPE *is not any one country, or collection of countries; the sick man of* EUROPE *is* EUROPE. *"* (Joel Kotkin)

SOCIAL DEMOCRACY

A political movement which advocates a strong role for the GOVERNMENT in the economy, and which assumes voters are too stupid to decide what to do with their MONEY. Social democracy therefore seeks to raise TAXES whenever possible; in a period of boom it is argued that the financially weaker classes have the RIGHT to a share in ECONOMIC GROWTH; in times of RECESSION they claim that more MONEY is needed to pay for WELFARE. See FABIAN SOCIETY, LIBERALS

SOCIAL SCIENCES

1. Sciences about society, such as history, psychology, sociology, ECONOMICS, politology, gender issues, and so on.
2. A GOVERNMENT programme for granting a university EDUCATION to students who are too useless at maths to become scientists or engineers, who don't have a good enough memory to study law, who hate the sight of blood so can't study medicine, and who are too weak and feeble to join the university rugby team.
3. Science fiction done earnestly; especially ECONOMIC SCIENCE.

Curious Fact: Societies can't be predicted in the long run

There have been many attempts to forecast the future. Some forecasters foresaw things that genuinely materialised over the course of history: carriages with no horses, telegraphs capable of sending and receiving colour pictures, portable wireless telephones, fast intercontinental air transport, memory crystals, digital watches, the atomic bomb. That sort of thing.

At the beginning of the 20th century, nobody predicted the world wars, the decline of the British Empire and the Austro-Hungarian monarchy, the Bolshevik revolution, the Holocaust, the Cold War, the decline of the Soviet empire, or GOVERNMENT expenditure reaching as much as half of GDP in many DEVELOPED countries.

Social developments have been totally unpredictable. No social scientist has ever been able to see anything important in advance. Not even by using advanced methods of mathematical modelling; see ACADEMIC ECONOMISTS.

This does not mean that the social sciences are completely worthless. History can certainly help us find some juicy mistakes to repeat, and economics provides us with a great example of how copying the natural sciences is unable to help us achieve anything much at all.

Curious Fact: Economies can't be predicted in the short run, either
"In our recent work we look at the record of professional forecasters in predicting RECESSIONS *over the period 2008-2012. There were a total of 88* RECESSIONS *over this period, where a* RECESSION *is defined as a year in which real* GDP *fell on a year-on-year basis in a given country.*

As shown, none of the 62 RECESSIONS *in 2008-09 was predicted as the previous year was drawing to a close. However, once the full realisation of the magnitude and breadth of the Great Recession became known, forecasters did predict, in September 2009, that eight countries would be in* RECESSION *in 2010, which turned out to be the* RIGHT *call in three of these cases. But the* RECESSIONS *in 2011-12 again came largely as a surprise to forecasters."*
(Hites Ahir, Prakash Loungani: *"Fail again? Fail better? Forecasts by economists during the Great Recession."* George Washington University Research Paper, 2014.)

Notable & Quotable
"Ask five economists and you'll get five different answers – six if one went to Harvard."
(Edgar R. Fiedler, American economist, 1929-2003)
"Barista is Italian for BA in liberal arts." (Robert Beau)

SOCIAL SECURITY *(in old age)*
Substitute for a proper income in old age provided by the STATE. The more you pay during your working life, the less you have when you need the MONEY most.
See PAY-AS-YOU-GO

SOCIALISM
1. The rule of the few who have the POWER to redistribute MONEY.
See OLIGARCHY
2. A theory which assumes that universal PROSPERITY can be achieved by putting the heaviest TAX burden upon the most productive subjects.
3. The belief that there are three classes of PEOPLE: the oppressed, the benefactors, and the ruling intellectual elite which governs the system and redistributes WEALTH. See also COMMUNISM, NATIONAL SOCIALISM
4. An economic system based on socialisation of private profits and the privatisation of GOVERNMENT losses.

SOCIALIST

A person who is self-confident enough to believe they are smarter than the market and therefore knows better than you how to spend your MONEY. See SPECULATOR, PUBLIC SERVANT

SOCIALIST STATE

A STATE which is run as a single giant CORPORATION, while all COMPETITION is banned and suppressed.

SOCIALISATION

A euphemism for expropriation or CONFISCATION.

SOCIETY

A large number of free individuals who share the common goal of pursuing their own individual HAPPINESS. See RIGHTS

Curious Fact: MARX was sometimes too Marxian for Marxist regimes

COMMUNIST regimes derived their legitimacy from the Marxian and allegedly scientific theory of history and SOCIETY; yet the above description of communist SOCIETY was so strikingly utopian that it was never taught in schools. Even school children would have seen that the original Marxian vision of COMMUNISM could never really work.

In case you are interested, for the definition of COMMUNISM that children were taught in communist countries, see COMMUNISM.

SOLIDARITY
1. Mutual support within a group of PEOPLE who share a common interest.
2. An excuse used by POLITICIANS for introducing ever more ENTITLEMENTS and HANDOUTS.

SOLVENCY
If you earn more than you spend, you are solvent. If you spend more than you earn, you are at RISK of being insolvent (skint, stony broke) one day. However, even if your bank account is empty at the moment, it does not mean you are insolvent. You may only be suffering from a CRISIS of liquidity, which will end as soon as your monthly salary arrives.

There is one important thing to note: if you are insolvent, nobody will rush to help you. If a BANK becomes insolvent, the GOVERNMENT will save it to avoid spreading systemic RISK. See LIQUIDITY, MORAL HAZARD

SOVEREIGN
A nation or STATE that acts independently and without outside interference. A description of European STATES before the inception of the EUROPEAN UNION. See SUZERAIN

SPECULATION
The buying and selling of EQUITIES, COMMODITIES, CURRENCIES or PROPERTY in the hope of making a profit; an easy way to get rich as long as you are smarter than the rest of the market—or to get poor if it's the other way round. See SPECULATOR

SPECULATOR

A person, usually male, who is self-confident enough to believe that he is smarter than the market and therefore knows better than you how to invest your MONEY. See SOCIALIST, OTHER PEOPLE'S MONEY

Curious Fact: SOCIALIST SPECULATORS

Look again at the definitions of a SPECULATOR and a SOCIALIST, and you'll see that they are practically identical. Does this mean SPECULATORS have a particular penchant for left-wing POLITICS?

To a large extent, yes—and not only SPECULATORS. There have been plenty of INVESTORS and entrepreneurs who have had SOCIALIST ideas. The famous (or infamous, depending on your point of view) George Soros has many ideas that could qualify him as a SOCIALIST. He believes, for instance, that a particular mood of the market may cause *"unsustainable and self-defeating* BOOM-*bust sequences or* BUBBLES*"*. The market must therefore be guarded by a GOVERNMENT body or a CENTRAL BANK. The idea of the GOVERNMENT being primary and the market secondary is, as it happens, another possible definition of SOCIALISM.

Ironically, the political left usually hate SPECULATORS and write them off as "predators" or "parasites". Many members of the various leftist organisations have no idea that they have been financed by the evil Soros!

SPURIOUS CORRELATION

A major source of mistakes in ECONOMICS. Most modern ACADEMIC ECONOMIC research is pursued as follows:

(1) Download some dataset or other. Anything you can lay your mouse upon. The larger the better. Use the phrase "Big Data" or any other phrase similarly in vogue.

(2) Torture the data using some kind of statistical software package until it sings. Find a correlation.

(3) Your paper is ready for publication. All you need to do now is invent some kind of theory, be it half-baked or completely raw, and ... bingo, you're done!

This is the easiest way to get your work published and earn a degree. It doesn't matter if the correlation is bogus or entirely fallacious and your work is therefore completely worthless. The worst thing that can happen is that your paper will be read by some BUREAUCRATS or CENTRAL BANKERS and your spurious conclusions will be implemented somewhere, somehow.

Curious Fact: Flies are no tourist attraction

The pseudo NOBEL PRIZE winner Ragnar Frisch used to warn his students of SPURIOUS CORRELATIONS by giving the following horrifying illustration. It can be observed that there is a high positive correlation between the number of flies on the western coast of Norway and the number of tourists visiting that region. From this observation, it is probably not such a good idea to attempt to promote tourism by breeding more flies. However, the phenomenon of SPURIOUS CORRELATION has a more intricate form, which is often much harder to discover. (Excerpt from the Nobel speech by Trygve Haavelmo.)

The most common (and most harmful) example of SPURIOUS CORRELATION is the so-called DEFLATION SPIRAL, which is the cause of the erroneous monetary policies pursued by many CENTRAL BANKS.

STATE

1. *"The STATE is a special organisation of force: it is an organization of violence for the suppression of some class."* (Karl MARX, *The STATE and REVOLUTION*)
2. *"The STATE is the great fiction through which everyone endeavours to live at the expense of everyone else."* (Frédéric Bastiat)
3. *"A city-STATE is a partnership of the free."* (Aristotle)
See DEBT, GOVERNMENT, SOCIALISM

STOCK EXCHANGE, STOCK MARKET

1. A financial marketplace where INVESTORS trade with EQUITIES and other securities; companies use it to raise capital by issuing stocks and BONDS.
2. A seriously huge casino for expert gamblers.

STOCK MARKET GURUS

The CXO Advisory Group LLC investigated 6,582 forecasts for the US STOCK MARKET offered publicly by 68 experts, bulls and bears employing technical, fundamental and sentiment indicators, between 2005 and 2012. The forecasts collected included those in the archives, and the oldest forecast in the sample was from the end of 1998. For the final report, CXO graded all of these forecasts.

The terminal accuracy was 46.9 per cent. The gurus therefore provided worse advice than tossing a coin. See P/E, SHILLER'S P/E, FORECASTING

SUBOPTIMAL EQUILIBRIUM

1. A situation characterised by failure beyond repair with little chance of escape without external assistance.
2. Deep shit.

See EMERGING MARKETS, EQUILIBRIUM, ZERO GROWTH

SUBPRIME CRISIS

When a BANK has a shortage of good (prime) DEBTORS, it starts to lend to the "subprime" or terrible ones; a situation which usually happens when the BANK has had too much MONEY to lend. See EXPANSIVE MONETARY POLICY, BAILOUT, MINSKY MOMENT

Curious Fact: Illegal immigrants don't make good DEBTORS
Starting in about 2000, subprime MORTGAGES became prevalent in the USA. In good faith, the FED set interest rates very low in order to spur ECONOMIC GROWTH. The artificially low interest rates caused the artificial growth of CREDIT as BANKS were massively providing MORTGAGES to clients with dubious CREDIT quality, including illegal immigrants. The FED followed the consumer PRICE INFLATION rather than the INFLATION of MORTGAGE CREDIT (which reached the annual rate of 11.8 per cent from 2000 to 2007). Therefore, it thought its policy would not cause a financial CRISIS. It was wrong. See MALINVESTMENTS

SUBSIDIES

1. An efficient way of helping certain industries (such as agriculture) or poor regions.
2. A legalised form of grand CORRUPTION.

Curious Fact: SUBSIDIES *are very harmful*
Since the 1980's, the largest recipients of EUROPEAN UNION (or EEC) SUBSIDIES have been SPAIN, GREECE, Ireland, PORTUGAL and the South of ITALY. The countries or regions hardest hit by the euro CRISIS have been SPAIN, GREECE, Ireland, PORTUGAL and the South of ITALY. Ouch.

Why the failure? SUBSIDIES work in unexpected and unintended ways. First, large SUBSIDIES induce CORRUPTION, which is bad for any economy. Secondly, SUBSIDIES increase costs, which is bad for COMPETITIVENESS. Thirdly, SUBSIDIES create false incentives and distort PRICES: goods are artificially cheaper (but sometimes more expensive) than they would be in an optimal EQUILIBRIUM. See SUBOPTIMAL EQUILIBRIUM

SUPPORT

A word that is prevalent in GOVERNMENT budget proposals across the world. One of the most expensive words in the dictionary, alongside SUBSIDIES and WELFARE.

SURPLUS VALUE

In the Marxist critique of CAPITALISM, surplus VALUE is that part of the total VALUE of the goods manufactured which CAPITALISTS keep for themselves; poor exploited workers don't get any of it. This is completely unjust, Marxists claim. Workers in CAPITALIST economies are constantly abused, which is supposedly a reason for inciting SOCIALIST REVOLUTION.

Curious Fact: There's no such thing as MARXIST ECONOMIC THEORY
The notion of SURPLUS VALUE is based upon the LABOUR THEORY OF VALUE. As you already know, the LABOUR THEORY OF VALUE is a theory which can, alas, be demolished by a mere three sandwiches (four in the case of difficult opponents). SURPLUS VALUE, therefore, does not exist—and neither does Marxist economic theory.

Oddly enough, therefore, the former Soviet RUSSIA and Maoist CHINA, together with large chunks of Asia, Africa and EUROPE, ran their economies according to a non-existent theory—a non-existent ECONOMIC model.

When it was no longer possible to conceal the demise of MARXISM, the Soviet bloc fell spectacularly, while CHINA quietly ditched SOCIALISM and reverted to CAPITALISM and a COMPETITION-based economy.

See MARXIST ECONOMY, MARGINAL THEORY OF VALUE, EMERGING MARKETS

SUZERAIN

A SOVEREIGN or state having control over another STATE that is internally autonomous. Historically a feudal overlord. Currently, most European countries are autonomous to some degree but controlled by a superstate entity. See SOVEREIGN

SYSTEMIC CORRUPTION

A form of GOVERNMENT in some countries.

SYSTEMIC RISK

The possibility that when things go wrong, they can go seriously wrong and affect pretty much everybody. See BANKS

SYSTEMATIC RISK

Not to be confused with SYSTEMIC RISK, systematic RISK is the fluctuation of EQUITY PRICES caused by factors that are common to all EQUITIES. Everybody loves systematic risk during a BULL MARKET; everybody is desperate during a BEAR MARKET. AMATEUR INVESTORS facing it for the first time become particularly terrified, to the point of selling their entire portfolio at the worst possible moment. See BETA COEFFICIENT, INVESTMENT DECISION CYCLE

TAXES, TAXATION, TAX RATES

1. *"Taxes are the price we pay for a civilized society."* (Attributed to Oliver Wendell Holmes, Jr. and now quoted by the American Internal Revenue Service above the entrance to their headquarters at 1111 Constitution Avenue, Washington DC.)

2. Theft, upgraded to GOVERNMENT policy.

3. Personal income TAX: a sky-high surcharge on wages and salaries, which in turn leads to a lower demand for labour, thereby resulting in high UNEMPLOYMENT.

4. Corporate income TAX: a fine on success.

5. VALUE-added TAX: the most powerful mechanism ever devised for extracting MONEY from PEOPLE.

6. PROPERTY TAX: a fine on being shrewd and prudent.

See TAX COMPETITION, FLAT TAX, PROGRESSIVE TAXATION, CONFISCATORY TAXATION, TAX HAVEN

Notable & Quotable
"The art of TAXATION *consists in so plucking the goose as to obtain the largest amount of feathers with the least possible amount of hissing.*"
(Jean-Baptiste Colbert)

TAX HAVEN

A courageous country or jurisdiction which can oppose the pressure of the great POWERS and keep its TAX RATES at competitively low levels.
See TAX COMPETITION

Curious Fact: The Swiss: the Indians of Europe

SWITZERLAND is a tax haven compared to most of its neighbours—GERMANY, FRANCE and ITALY. GERMANY is especially jealous about the money of wealthy Germans flowing into SWITZERLAND. If you go to SWITZERLAND by car, your can be stopped and searched by German police. Peer Steinbrück, the former German minister of finance, once threatened to "whip" the Swiss like children, and then compared them to Indians giving up under pressure from the financial cavalry. Steinbrück infuriated the Swiss to such a degree that a member of the Swiss parliament has called for a boycott of German cars.

TAX COMPETITION

As in other fields of human activity, TAXATION is also subject to COMPETITION. Depending on your worldview, you may consider it:

1. A harmful thing which undermines attempts to raise more GOVERNMENT income for funding WELFARE and subsidies.

2. A good thing which makes GOVERNMENTS prudent about PUBLIC EXPENDITURE and relieves taxpayers of excessive burden.

See TAX HAVEN, COMPETITION

TAXPAYER

1. An abstract deity worshipped by POLITICIANS shortly before ELECTIONS.

2. A defenceless serf who covers all of the expenses incurred by the GOVERNMENT, including WELFARE, SUBSIDIES and CORRUPTION (with the notable exception of the expenses that are covered by DEBT).

THIRD WORLD COUNTRIES

In the Cold War years, DEVELOPED COUNTRIES used to be considered the first world, SOCIALIST countries the second world, and, of course, the impoverished countries of Africa, Asia, and Latin America the third world.

Over the years, second-world countries largely dropped to third-world standards, as did certain territories in first-world countries. See MIDDLE EAST. Meanwhile, the original third-world countries have been rebranded as EMERGING MARKETS.

TIGER ECONOMY

A label attached to a country which is rapidly advancing towards a banking or CURRENCY CRISIS. We heard about the Asian Tigers (Hong Kong, Indonesia, Korea, Malaysia, Singapore, Thailand) before the Asian CRISIS of 1997, about the Celtic Tiger (Ireland) before the crisis of 2008, the Baltic Tigers (Latvia, Lithuania, Estonia) at the same time, and, most notably, Iceland, which was proudly labelled the Nordic Tiger shortly before its banking system folded and the country became insolvent. Most European economies, however, were struck by a crisis without being known as tigers.
See SICK MAN

TRADE WARS

If you want victory over your competitor, you will cut PRICES—if you can. This is called COMPETITION. Or you can convince your GOVERNMENT to impose customs on imports and to erect trade barriers. This is called a trade WAR. If your competitor doesn't want to allow you access to its markets as well, there is a reason to start a real WAR. A far nastier thing indeed.
See WORLD WAR I

TRADER

1. A person, usually male, whose employer believes he is smarter than the market, and is therefore allowed to play with his employer's MONEY (which is, in fact, the employer's clients' MONEY).
See also INVESTMENT BANK, SOCIALIST, QUANT
2. A gambler who uses EQUITIES, COMMODITIES or a foreign CURRENCY market as a casino.
See WALL STREET

Curious Fact: Hormone-driven markets

A study from Cambridge University bolsters existing evidence that supports the primacy of male hormones in driving a market full of traders, as levels of testosterone and cortisol fluctuate in relation to one another. In research published in the Proceedings of the National Academy of Sciences, former Wall Street trader John Coates found a 68 per cent increase in average levels of cortisol, a stress hormone, among a group of CITY of London traders over eight days of increasingly volatile trading.

"There is a powerful physiological mechanism at work in the markets, and no one—not the traders, not the RISK managers, not the policy makers—is aware of it", Coates told the Financial Times. *"This assumption, mostly hidden from view, underlies almost every economic model, and, it turns out, every indicator of market sentiment."*
(Coates J., Gurnell M., Fletcher P.C., Graggaber J., Schaffner M., and Page L.: Cortisol shifts financial risk preference. PNAS, 2014)

TROIKA

Originally, troikas were special tribunals operated by the NKVD security agency in RUSSIA, especially during the STALIN era. A troika rarely delivered a sentence other than death or being sent to a Gulag.

Today, Troika (with a capital T) is a commission constituted from among representatives of the EUROPEAN UNION, the European CENTRAL BANK and the International Monetary Fund to oversee the weaker member STATES of the EUROZONE. Yes indeed, the above institutions have a rather odd sense of humour.

TULIP MANIA

A memorable speculative BUBBLE in the Netherlands which peaked between 1636 and 1637. Many speculators went broke after the BUBBLE burst. This experience may lead to the optimistic conclusion that foolishness is not a trait unique to the PEOPLE of the modern era.

TUNNELLING
Asset stripping carried out in macroeconomic dimensions, especially in EMERGING MARKETS.

UNEMPLOYMENT

A mass of PEOPLE PRICED out of the LABOUR market by an artificially high PRICE of LABOUR due to excessive income and payroll TAX RATES.

Curious Fact: When UNEMPLOYMENT *was low in Italy, France and* SPAIN

In 1970, UNEMPLOYMENT in FRANCE was at 2.5 per cent, in ITALY at 5.3 per cent, and in SPAIN at 2.4 per cent. The total average wage TAX burden was at 25.4%, 27.3%, and 17.5%, respectively. Compare this with current figures. Hiking the LABOUR TAX burden never fails to increase UNEMPLOYMENT.

UNITARY STATE

Unlike federalism, a unitary form of GOVERNMENT knows only one CAPITAL city, one legislative body and one GOVERNMENT. Consequently, the only chance TAXPAYERS within the state have of choosing a less TAX-oppressive jurisdiction is to leave it. See TAX COMPETITION

UNLIMITED WANTS

See DESIRE, GREED, SEX, MARRIAGE, LUXURY GOODS, MISTRESS

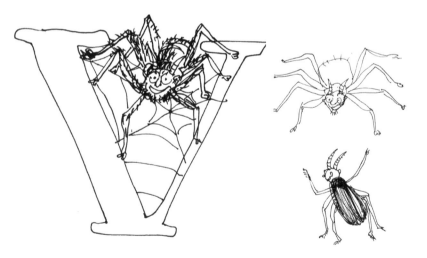

VALUE

The regard in which something is held; the importance, worth, or usefulness of something.

VOLATILITY

A measure of the price fluctuation of stocks and BONDS which conceals the true meaning and nature of RISK. See BETA COEFFICIENT, RATING

VOTING RIGHTS

The right to vote is a valuable asset granted to any adult citizen of a democratic country by the CONSTITUTION. That which comes free, however, is little VALUED, which is why voters tend to exchange their precious political POWER for cheap promises.

WALL STREET

A short and relatively unimportant street in downtown Manhattan; the address of the New York Stock Exchange, whose real centre is in a nondescript building in Brooklyn. An archetypal symbol of MONEY and POWER, and of the abuse of both. See TRADER

Notable & Quotable
"WALL STREET: *A symbol for sin for every devil to rebuke. That* WALL STREET *is a den of thieves is a belief that serves every unsuccessful thief in place of a hope in Heaven.*" (Ambrose Bierce, The Devil's Dictionary)

Curious Fact: Testosterone therapy for WALL STREET TRADERS
The male hormone testosterone has become the unlikely drug of choice
for WALL STREET TRADERS seeking to give themselves the edge over their
PROFESSIONAL rivals. New York clinics have reported a rise in treatment
for "testosterone deficiency", sometimes known as andropause. Many workers
in this male-dominated industry are hoping that a boost of the hormone will
help them perform better at work and put in longer hours.

Dr. Lionel Bissoon, who provided the hormone therapy, added: *"If you're
going to be trading on* WALL STREET *or dealing with large sums of* MONEY, *you
had better be confident. The man who is wishy-washy is not going to be successful."*

WAR
A major event that hugely stimulates ECONOMIC GROWTH until everything
is razed to the ground. When the war ends, the war DEBT burden and high
TAX RATES undermine ECONOMIC stability in peacetime. See POLITICS

Curious Fact: Spitfire production boosted the British economy
The British economy grew at its fastest pace ever in **1940**, when it galloped
by **11.3** per cent in INFLATION-adjusted terms. Obviously, this type of ECONOMIC
GROWTH is not associated with improving living standards. The production
of Spitfires and other weapons was simply a matter of survival.

Notable & Quotable
"War doesn't determine who's RIGHT *– only who's left."* (Bertrand Russell)

WAR DEBT
If your country wins the WAR, you and your children must pay for its DEBT;
if your country loses, it is declared bankrupt and you are DEBT-free!
See GREAT BRITAIN, GERMANY

Curious Fact: The Biggest DEBT *Transgressor*
In an interview published in Spiegel Online on **21** June **2011**, Professor
Albrecht Ritschl of the LONDON School of ECONOMICS presented the following
frequently forgotten facts:

- Spiegel Online: If there was a list of the worst global BANKRUPTCIES in history, where would GERMANY rank?
- Ritschl: GERMANY is king when it comes to DEBT. Based on the amount of
losses compared to ECONOMIC performance, GERMANY was the biggest debt
transgressor of the **20**th century.

- Spiegel Online: The GERMANY of today is considered the embodiment of stability. How many times has GERMANY become insolvent in the past?
- Ritschl: That depends on how you do the maths. During the past century alone, though, at least three times. After the first default during the 1930's, the USA gave GERMANY a "haircut" in 1953, reducing its DEBT problem to practically nothing. GERMANY has been in a very good position ever since, even as other Europeans were forced to endure the burdens of WORLD WAR II and the consequences of the German occupation. GERMANY even had a period of non-payment in 1990.
- Spiegel Online: Really? A default?
- Ritschl: Yes, then-chancellor Helmut Kohl refused at the time to implement changes to the LONDON Agreement on German External DEBTS of 1953. Under the terms of the agreement, in the event of a reunification, the issue of German reparations payments from WORLD WAR II would be newly regulated. The only demand made was that a small remaining sum be paid, but we're talking about minimal sums here. With the exception of compensation paid out to forced laborers, GERMANY did not pay any reparations after 1990–and neither did it pay off the loans and occupation costs it pressed out of the countries it had occupied during WORLD WAR II. Not to the GREEKS, either.
(Source: Spiegel Online International, 21 June 2011)

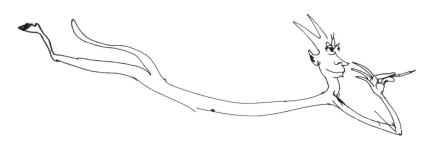

WASHINGTON CONSENSUS
1. A set of policy rules and recommendations conceived in 1989. It includes: fiscal policy discipline; the redirection of PUBLIC SPENDING from subsidies to primary EDUCATION, health care and infrastructure INVESTMENT; broadening the TAX base and adopting moderate marginal TAX rates; INTEREST RATES that are market determined and moderate; competitive CURRENCY exchange rates; trade and foreign INVESTMENT liberalisation; the privatisation of STATE-owned enterprises; the abolition of regulations that restrict COMPETITION; and legal security for PROPERTY RIGHTS.

In other words, the Washington Consensus represents an attempt to transfer the practice of DEVELOPED countries to EMERGING MARKETS.
2. According to SOCIALISTS, the root cause of much of the world's evil and hardship.
See NEOLIBERALISM

WEALTH
1. All forms of MONEY, SECURITIES, PROPERTY, and LUXURY GOODS.
2. A special type of magnet which attracts AUDITORS, tax inspectors, lawyers and prospective MISTRESSES.

WELFARE
1. Archaic sense: well-being, health, good health, HAPPINESS, comfort, security, safety, protection, PROSPERITY, profit, good, success, fortune, good fortune, advantage, interest, prosperousness, successfulness. (Oxford English Dictionary)
2. Expensive GOVERNMENT programmes in DEVELOPED ECONOMIES resulting in mass UNEMPLOYMENT and disastrous levels of GOVERNMENT DEBT.

Notable & Quotable
"The WELFARE STATE *is a soft prison, a system of induced incapacity, to the benefit of the wardens."* (Anthony Esolen)

Curious Fact: No erosion of the WELFARE STATE
The political left across the globe constantly cries and laments about the alleged "erosion of the WELFARE STATE". This is nonsense. The WELFARE STATE has never been larger or more voracious than it is now.

In fact, the UNITED KINGDOM spent 23.8 per cent of its GDP on social protection in 2013. In 1990, the share of GDP spent on welfare amounted to only 16.7 per cent. In 1980 (the pre-Thatcher era), it was 16.5 per cent of GDP. Where is the alleged erosion?

Similar numbers can be shown for the USA and for most DEVELOPED COUNTRIES, as well as for some EMERGING MARKETS.

WIRTSCHAFTSWUNDER
The German word for "economic miracle" denoting the period from 1948 to the early 1970's. The era of strong ECONOMIC GROWTH and negligible UNEMPLOYMENT in GERMANY which ended with the expansion of the WELFARE STATE from the mid 1970's. See WORLD WAR II

WORLD WAR I

Also called The Great War. Started as a trade conflict. GERMANY felt she needed access to international markets. FRANCE and Britain were reluctant to remove trade barriers. GERMANY finally decided to use force, including poison gas and flamethrowers, to open the doors for business. Bad idea, as it turned out. GERMANY needed one more world conflict to realise that it's cheaper to buy enemy STATES than to beat them.
See EUROPEAN UNION, MADE IN, PROTECTIONISM, TRADE WARS, WORLD WAR II

WORLD WAR II

A major military conflict won by GERMANY, which achieved two key victories: access to international markets, and the cancellation of almost all of her GOVERNMENT DEBT, including the WORLD WAR I reparations. This enabled GERMANY to cut TAXES and maintain a low-inflation hard CURRENCY during the post-war period—the Deutschmark. The UNITED KINGDOM, the UNITED STATES and FRANCE, on the other hand, ended up with GOVERNMENT DEBTS of over 260, 110, and 230 per cent of GDP respectively. To be more accurate, according to BANK of England statistics, British DEBT amounted to 262.9 per cent of GDP in 1946. The winner's burden. See WAR DEBT, WIRTSCHAFTSWUNDER

WORST-CASE SCENARIO

A usual chapter in ECONOMIC analyses, which shows how little imagination analysts usually have.

XENOPHOBIA

The fear that foreigners from barbaric countries will crush your motor industry, manufacture your goods, inflate the PRICE of your PROPERTIES, gather your daughters to their bosom, and sell you kebabs while patiently listening to your endless lamentations.

YIELD
BOND yield: The equivalent of the interest rate for BONDS, usually a low single-digit figure, which is unlikely to win the uneven fight with INFLATION over the next ten, twenty or even thirty years.

Dividend yield: A meagre portion of corporate after-TAX profits distributed among shareholders.

Rental yield: What your greedy landlord believes is not enough to cover expenses.

ZERO GROWTH

In the theory of zero growth, PEOPLE should reduce unnecessary production and CONSUMPTION to achieve a STATE of equilibrium and devote more time to the family, the arts, ecology, the community, and well-being in general. In fact, zero growth usually brings about SUBOPTIMAL EQUILIBRIUM, leading to UNEMPLOYMENT, stress and POVERTY. See DEGROWTH

A XENOPHOBE'S CONCISE ATLAS OF THE WORLD

Only superficial, ignorant people hate other countries and cultures without reason. Sophisticated, educated people, on the other hand, find plenty to complain about in every country in the world. Including their own, of course. We live in an age of non-discrimination, which obviously means that genuine modern-day xenophobia includes that pertaining to your own nation.

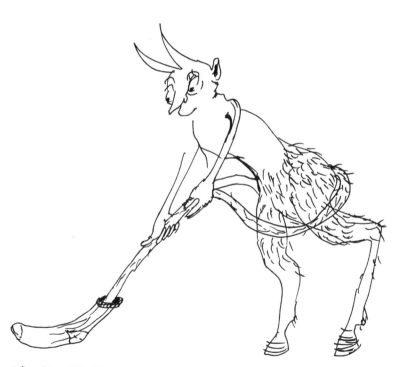

The Devil's Fashion Collection

AFGHANISTAN
The recent history of this country shows, pretty convincingly, that Allah dislikes uneducated gunmen—even those who claim to be fighting in his name.

Devil's question: What would the Prophet say?

AUSTRIA
The Habsburg dynasty struck upon a winning formula: conquer your neighbours, live off their TAXES and workforce and bleed them dry for the next three hundred years. You are then in a position to boast about your prosperity. This formula worked brilliantly until an aged monarch decided to jump into bed with the perpetually-losing GERMANY and kick off WORLD WAR I. Interestingly enough, even after two bitter military defeats, Austria has remained one of the richest—and most complacent—countries in EUROPE.

Devil's question: Is the EUROPEAN UNION a bit like AUSTRIA-HUNGARY? Do all its member states feel comfortable being part of it?

Notable & Quotable
"I came from a SOCIALIST country where the GOVERNMENT controls the economy. It's a place where you can hear 18-year-old kids talking about their pension. But me, I wanted more. I wanted to be the best. Individualism like that is incompatible with SOCIALISM. So I felt I had to come to America."
(Arnold Schwarzenegger)

BELGIUM
Belgium is a country which once had no GOVERNMENT for 589 days. But at least it could still make chocolate.

Devil's message: Perhaps having a GOVERNMENT isn't as great as it's cooked up to be.

BRAZIL

The country of the future, which will probably remain the country of the future well into the distant future. A country with some of the most rigid and BUREAUCRATIC LABOUR and business laws. It takes 128 days to start up a company in BRAZIL; the average time in DEVELOPED COUNTRIES is 11 days. It takes 2700 hours to complete a corporate TAX form in BRAZIL, compared to 175 hours in DEVELOPED COUNTRIES.

Devil's question: Is this the reason DEVELOPED COUNTRIES *are developed and* EMERGING MARKETS *rarely fully emerge?*

CALIFORNIA

A state that is outpacing the rest of the USA in producing both MILLIONAIRES and food-stamp recipients.

Devil's message: Only Hawaii and Oregon have higher income TAX RATES *for top earners; only Oregon and Washington State have a higher minimum wage per hour (as of 2014). Maybe the less well-off are more vulnerable to a high* TAX *burden than are the rich.*

CHAD

The country which trumps even DENMARK in terms of its upper personal income TAX RATE, but regrettably not in terms of HAPPINESS.

Devil's message: Wealth is not built on high TAX RATES. *Even* DENMARK *had to get rich first, and only then impose high* TAXES. *Chad chose the opposite approach, and it hasn't worked.*

CHINA

China's recent history proves that COMMUNISM, famine and even cannibalism, when replaced by CAPITALISM, can be followed by an extended period of healthy ECONOMIC GROWTH.
Devil's message: Without COMMUNISM, *China would have been the world's strongest superpower decades ago. (Devil's question: Should the West be happy about that?)*

CZECH REPUBLIC *(formerly part of Czechoslovakia, and before that part of Austria-Hungary)*

A country with a certain amount of know-how in the assembly of cars and the disassembly of federative STATES and CURRENCY unions.

Devil's question: Why hasn't this country introduced an official single-word name for itself yet? A perfectly serviceable one already exists: Bohemia.

DENMARK

A wonderful nation which bears the heaviest TAX burden in the world, yet still remains at the top of most HAPPINESS rankings.

Devil's message: Even a very high tax burden seems bearable if the GOVERNMENT is competent and not corrupt.

FRANCE

France invented the motto 'Liberté, Égalité, Fraternité'. Liberté stands for the heaviest TAX burden in EUROPE (outside DENMARK). Égalité means the absolute rule of graduates of the ENA, the GOVERNMENT-run school for BUREAUCRATS. Fraternité refers to the incessant clashes between French natives and immigrants from Africa, the Middle East and the rest of the world. (It is interesting to note that Europeans settling in other continents have generally been called 'colonists', while non-Europeans settling in EUROPE are never referred to as such even though the process is exactly the same.) See COLONIALISM

Devil's question: Does "liberté" mean human RIGHTS or handouts?

GERMANY

Germany was divided for centuries and produced Dürer, Holbein, Haydn, Bach, Schiller, Goethe, Gauss, and Leibniz, a list which represents a mere fraction of the country's greatest geniuses.

It was then united, and produced Wilhelm II, HYPERINFLATION, the worst financial CRISIS in human history, Hitler, Goebbels, and Himmler, a list which represents a mere fraction of the country's most terrible failures.

It was then divided again and West Germany produced the WIRTSCHAFTS-WUNDER.

Germany then united once more and produced the EURO and Angela Merkel.

Devil's message: Germany is so fabulous it's a shame there's only one of them.

Devil's other message: Germany last won a war in 1871. It then needed to lose two world wars in order to find out that it's cheaper and easier simply to buy EUROPE rather than to try to beat it.
See MADE IN GERMANY

GREAT BRITAIN

The country which invented the steam engine, the industrial revolution and CLASSICAL LIBERALISM, only to be economically outperformed by DEBT-free GERMANY after WORLD WAR II. See UNITED KINGDOM

GREECE

An ancient nation formerly at the vanguard of European civilisation; in a sense, it still is.

Devil's message: The crisis taking place in Greece since 2009 could happen to any European WELFARE STATE, sooner or later.

HUNGARY

A country with a tradition of expelling its most excellent brains, such as John von Neumann, Theodor Karman, Joseph Pulitzer, Edward Teller, and András Gróf (aka Andy Grove of Intel). This is good news for the USA, but not perhaps such good news for Hungary.

Devil's question: How would Hungary have fared if it had retained and utilised all of its exiled brainpower?

INDIA
Proof that a zero growth economy is possible. All you need is CORRUPTION and a debilitatingly large BUREAUCRACY. Interestingly, India has the world's longest CONSTITUTION, which runs to a whopping 146,385 words—almost 19 times longer than the US CONSTITUTION.

Devil's message: The most heinous crime of COLONIALISM was exporting half-baked economic ideas—and bureaucracy—to DEVELOPING COUNTRIES.

ISRAEL
Established in 1948, the modern STATE of Israel seems to have demonstrated that the Jewish nation produces better warriors than businesspeople—contrary to most established clichés. Only in the 1990's, when Israel rid itself of the SOCIALIST legacy of its founders, did its economy start to flourish.

Devil's message: Genesis, the story of the world's first start-up, still remains an inspiration.

ITALY
The modern STATE of Italy has been heavily indebted ever since its unification in 1861. Brief periods of lower levels of DEBT have occurred only rarely, as a consequence of DEFAULTS or DEBT forgiveness, particularly after WORLD WAR II.

Devil's question: Knowing the country's history, could you—when stone-cold sober and in full command of all your faculties—even begin to think of investing your precious cash in Italian GOVERNMENT BONDS?

JAPAN
A DEVELOPED MARKET which has seen an enviable level of technological progress. Japan was nonetheless hit by the financial and banking CRISIS of 1990 and has never fully recovered. Japan's stock market thus defies all the rules concerning the recommended INVESTMENT HORIZON. Twenty-five years after it peaked in 1989, the Nikkei equity index has been well below (up to 60 per cent below) its historical maximum. Ouch.

Devil's message: Be very careful about investing in economies with overbloated BANKS! (Unfortunately, it's a little difficult to find a DEVELOPED MARKET which doesn't have an overbloated banking sector.)

LUXEMBOURG, LIECHTENSTEIN, MONACO, SAN MARINO
Four minuscule STATES which all prove that small is beautiful (and prosperous); EU, take note.

Devil's question: Luxembourg's politicians are well known for being pro-EU; are they planning to build a Luxembourg-centred empire by stealth?

MIDDLE EAST
A geographical area which includes the Arab STATES, Israel, Iran and Turkey. These territories used to be known as the Near East. That name is, however, no longer used in modern English due to possible confusion with a number of other locations, such as Brussels, Poland, Romania, and Tower Hamlets.

PORTUGAL
A small European nation whose language is spoken in Brazil and a few African countries, including Angola, Cape Verde, Guinea-Bissau, Mozambique and São Tomé and Príncipe. When the European financial crisis hit Portugal, it was a blessing for the Portuguese to have a few former colonies in which their language is still spoken.

ROMANIA
A Balkan country that derives its name from the ancient Roman Empire, not from the ethnic minority of the Roma PEOPLE as some Britons think—much to the chagrin of the non-Roma Romanians who fervently believe that the ancient Romans were their ancestors.

RUSSIA
Some believe that the history of Russia proves that SOCIALISM represents the longest and most expensive shortcut from CAPITALISM to CAPITALISM. Others hold that it's been the longest and most expensive shortcut from feudalism to feudalism.

Devil's question: Did you know that the young cadres destined to become OLIGARCHS were hand-picked and trained in business and finance by the KGB as early as the 1980's?

Notable & Quotable
"Putin's economic policy: when the banker in Monopoly mixes the BANK's MONEY with his own till the two entities become one." (Philip Schuyler)

SPAIN

Spain once destroyed its economy by allowing itself to receive too much stolen gold from Columbus; that caused INFLATION and a loss of COMPETITIVENESS. Spain has recently repeated this feat by allowing itself to receive too much CREDIT from the European CENTRAL BANK.

Devil's message: MONEY *does not make a country rich. Not even gold. It is brainpower and hard work that lead to* PROSPERITY. *No shortcuts. Sorry.*

SWITZERLAND

Everybody knows Switzerland as a country which is politically stable to the point of boredom. Interestingly, the word "putsch" comes from Swiss German. Switzerland used to be a collection of warring banana republics (with no bananas) until it replicated UNITED STATES-style federalism with its new CONSTITUTION of 1848.

Devil's question: When will the EUROPEAN UNION *catch on to the fact that the Swiss are good at something other than* BANKS, *chocolate and watches?*

SWEDEN

The Swedish term "kungliga svenska avundsjukan" translates as royal Swedish ENVY; the word "royal" is not directly related to the royal family—it merely makes the expression stronger. (Interestingly, the word "avundsjukan" is a composite: avund = ENVY, sjukan = disease.)

Apparently, royal Swedish envy is more powerful than the Royal Swedish Navy, judging by the volume of GOVERNMENT tax income and WELFARE expenditure.

Devil's question: Doesn't managing to survive under such a heavy tax burden make Sweden a truly great nation? See ASTRID LINDGRÉN

TEXAS

Texas used to be an independent republic which was diplomatically recognised by the USA and a few other countries. The republic only existed, however, for nine years, from 1836 to 1845. The Republic of Texas was highly indebted and exposed to the threat of another WAR with Mexico. It therefore chose to join the USA, and formally lost its SOVEREIGNTY in 1846. A few years later, in 1850, Texas ceded about a third of its territory in exchange for the sum of $10 million, which paid for its DEBT of roughly the same size. That was about 29 dollars per square kilometre (75 dollars per square mile) of land. The mother of all fire sales.

Devil's message: Don't take on too much DEBT; *invest in* PROPERTY!

UNITED KINGDOM, *(UK)*

Usually known simply as the UK. Formerly, in a less modest age, referred to as GREAT BRITAIN.

Devil's question: When you register a UK-based company at Companies House, you have a choice: your business address can be in either the United Kingdom or GREAT BRITAIN. *They are both the same country—which of the two names do you prefer?*

UNITED STATES OF AMERICA, *(USA)*

Home of the brave and land of the free. But also the land of obesity, the ECONOMICS of CONSUMPTION and a hugely negative trade balance. Fortunately, the USA has also been a country which has given a home to the poor and homeless masses, including, among many others, Nikola Tesla, Alexander Graham Bell, Albert Einstein, John von Neumann, András Gróf (see HUNGARY), Pierre Omidyar (see FRANCE) and Sergei Brin (see RUSSIA).

Devil's message: Immigration is a great way to build a great nation—unless it's motivated by WELFARE *and free food stamps.*

VATICAN

Make sin tradable goods and invest the proceeds from selling indulgences in PROPERTY: a great idea.

Devil's message: Only God is omniscient; the rest of us have to settle for being merely curious about certain rather delicate financial affairs of the Papal STATE.

VENEZUELA

Venezuelans have convinced themselves that the Eastern European experiment with MARXISM went wrong only because Eastern Europeans were too backward and uneducated to understand Karl MARX properly. Only when a lack of toilet paper (and other staple items) in Venezuelan shops proved that a MARXIST ECONOMY had failed yet again did PEOPLE fill the streets in protest.

Devil's question: When will Western Marxists make sense of what has been going on in the real world?

ZIMBABWE

Originally called Rhodesia, the country was built on racial discrimination that favoured whites. Years after gaining independence, it is once more based on racism, this time aimed against white farmers. Clearly, racism (even anti-white racism) is not good for the economy.

Devil's message: The 'DISMAL SCIENCE' *of economics implies that all human beings are created equal; a disrespect for that rule is universally harmful.*

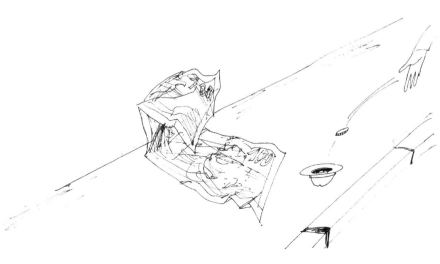

A PANOPTIC OF LUMINARIES
AND THEIR INFAMOUS FINANCIAL FIASCOS

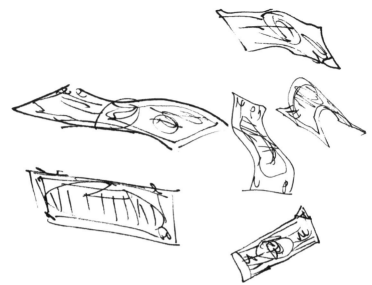

Rudolf von Havenstein printed enough money to make every German billionaire.

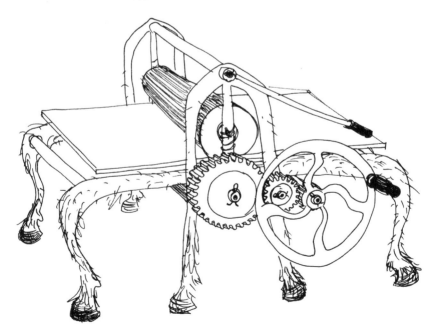

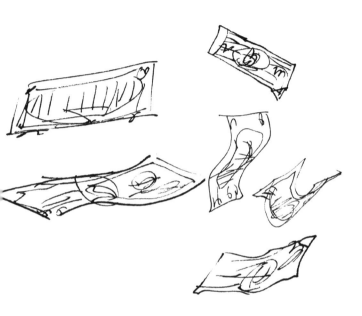

How do you know if somebody is a really important person? By the number of really big mistakes they have made. Only boringly average people live their lives without committing major errors, miscalculations and blunders. Real greatness is in failure. Only those who never achieved anything never got anything wrong.

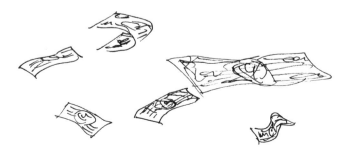

ATTLEE, *Clement*

Attlee is accused of, or praised for, turning British politics sharply to the left. He was largely responsible for NATIONALISATION and the extremely high TAX RATES of the post-war period. This, together with massive GOVERNMENT DEBT, has undoubtedly caused the lasting post-war decline of the British economy.

But Attlee is still ranked highly by the British public for having established public services such as the NHS. In some polls he even beats CHURCHILL and Margaret THATCHER.

Devil's message: Not even the civilised, Fabian-style British variety of SOCIALISM has worked properly, but a lot of PEOPLE still seem to like the idea.

Notable & Quotable
"A sheep in sheep's clothing."
"A modest man, who has much to be modest about."
"An empty taxi arrived at 10 Downing Street, and when the door was opened, Atlee got out."
(Winston CHURCHILL on Clement ATLEE)

BRÜNING, *Alfred*

Brüning was a prototype democratic and very fine POLITICIAN who made terrible decisions while maintaining the widely acknowledged principles of good economic policy according to the STATE of knowledge at the time. Having pursued the CONSERVATIVE policies of a strong CURRENCY and a balanced budget, he refused to devalue the Reichsmark when he needed to and hiked TAXES in the middle of the worst financial CRISIS of the century. Bad idea. The economic CRISIS that followed paved the way for Adolf Hitler.

Brüning inadvertently strengthened Hitler's position; had he followed less orthodox economic policies, NATIONAL SOCIALISM may never have become a genuine force.

Devil's message: Hiking TAXES slows down the economy—and a slow economy is a breeding ground for discontent.

CHURCHILL, *Winston Spencer*

The great statesman was a much better military strategist than economic policy maker. As Chancellor of the Exchequer in the 1920's, he carried out monetary policy in a strictly CONSERVATIVE manner and this resulted, eventually, in the general strike. This in turn radicalised the LABOUR Party, which won a decisive victory in the parliamentary ELECTIONS of 1945 and began nationalising British industry. Oh well. Only irrelevant nobodies make no mistakes at all.

Devil's message: A strong CURRENCY *is great, but not at the expense of employment and* CONSUMPTION.

CLINTON, *Bill*

The US president who invented the catchphrase "It's the economy, stupid." The American economy was, admittedly, in pretty good shape during his two terms in office. Clinton avoided anything RADICAL and except for relatively moderate TAX increases tended to leave the economy humming happily along all by itself. The Clinton era was also marked by the recently won Cold WAR (thanks to Ronald Reagan). The 'peace dividend' alleviated Federal expenditure as American military outlay fell to 3.45 per cent of GDP in 2001 from the Reagan-era peak of 6.84 per cent in 1986.

Having profited from Reagan's victory, Clinton may have gradually eliminated the Federal DEBT. Some American economists even worried that Treasury BONDS would disappear as a MONETARY POLICY tool. As one research paper published by the Federal Reserve System put it: *"A substantial decline in the outstanding stock of Treasury* DEBT *would pose a major challenge to policymakers."* According to a forecast made by the Congressional Budget Office (CBO) in 2000, the Federal DEBT was expected to fall below 10 per cent of GDP in 2015.

But Clinton made one very serious mistake. By paying too much attention to his reproductive organ, he had insufficient energy to deal with a series of terrorist attacks: the World Trade Center (1993), the US Embassy in Saudi Arabia (1995), the Khobar Towers in Saudi Arabia (1996), the US embassies in Kenya and Tanzania (1998), and the USS Cole (2000). Due to Clinton's indecisive foreign and security policy, terrorists concluded that the USA was a country of spoilt rich weaklings who are too timid to put up a fight. This conclusion has had deep and lasting consequences. Among others, the Federal DEBT is now around ten times greater than the CBO forecast of 2000.

Devil's message: It's not only the economy, Bill.

DUBČEK, *Alexander*

A Czechoslovak COMMUNIST politician who believed that SOCIALISM and the FREEDOM to pursue individual HAPPINESS were somehow compatible. They weren't.

In 1968, Dubček was ousted by orthodox followers of real SOCIALISM. But SOCIALISM had its consequences. It impoverished the country more than two WORLD WARS did. In 1989, the average wage of a Czechoslovak worker was equivalent to a mere $850 per annum. Back in 1946, Czechoslovakia had been wealthier than AUSTRIA. See RIGHTS

Devil's message: SOCIALISM *doesn't work. It simply does not.*

EISENHOWER, *Dwight David "Ike"*

This highly successful military strategist and statesman made mistakes, too. He kept marginal income TAX at the wartime confiscatory level of 91 per cent right up until he left office in 1961. Nonetheless, due largely to rapid MORTGAGE and private CREDIT growth, the 1950's were a period of PROSPERITY and low UNEMPLOYMENT. Some presidents simply get lucky—but don't try doing this at home.

Devil's message: Only if you are running the world's strongest economy with robust growth momentum can you afford to impose exorbitant TAXES *—and then only for a limited term. No other economy could bear the same burden.*

FAMA, *Eugene*

A pseudo NOBEL PRIZE laureate. Awarded in 2013 for the EFFICIENT MARKET HYPOTHESIS, which STATES that STOCK MARKET BUBBLES never really appear and we are only dreaming if we think we have spotted one. Fama has held this opinion since the 1960's. *"I don't even know what a* BUBBLE *means,"* Fama said recently. Being prized for knowing the patently obvious is quite a feat, but to receive eight million Swedish kronor for not knowing something self-evident is clearly a stroke of genius.

Unfortunately, INVESTORS who took Fama too seriously suffered heavy losses when the NASDAQ stock index fell (no, collapsed) by 78 per cent between 2000 and 2002. Believers of Fama's infamous hypothesis took another beating in 2007 when the credit BUBBLE burst.

Devil's message: Blind faith in ACADEMIC ECONOMISTs *comes at a high* PRICE.

FORD, *Henry*

Henry Ford originally established the Detroit Automobile Company. After just two years, having produced just 20 cars, he filed for BANKRUPTCY. He took heed of this lesson, however. In 1903, when he created the Ford Motor Company, he started what would become one of the greatest American companies of all time.

Devil's message: Going bankrupt can provide more valuable EDUCATION *than most* BUSINESS SCHOOLS.

FRIEDMAN, *Milton*

As an important theorist and influential advocate of PRIVATISATION, Friedman neglected the fact that it must be done honestly to work well. In RUSSIA and many post-communist countries, PRIVATISATION created a small class of wealthy OLIGARCHS, but was otherwise only a mixed success.

Devil's message: The devil is in the DETAIL. *Honesty is one such small* DETAIL, *and often neglected.*

GANDHI, *Mahatma*

Gandhi won his country's independence by peaceful means, but his peculiar views on the economy sentenced millions of PEOPLE to lasting POVERTY. See NEHRU

Devil's message: Independence is great, but PEOPLE *have to eat too.*

GREENSPAN, *Alan*

Long-serving chairman of the board of governors of the FED, in office from 1987 to 2006, and formerly known as the Maestro. Until 2008, he was credited with the robust ECONOMIC GROWTH and low UNEMPLOYMENT enjoyed by the American economy. After 2008, he was blamed for the CREDIT BUBBLE; the BOOM turned to bust and high UNEMPLOYMENT. His principal mistake was believing that the consumer PRICE index was an adequate tool for measuring INFLATION.

Devil's message: As soon as they start calling you Maestro, retire. Immediately.

HAVENSTEIN, *Rudolf von*

The president of the Reichsbank (German CENTRAL BANK) who was in office during the HYPERINFLATION episode of 1921-1923. During his term, the price of the US dollar skyrocketed from 4.2 to 4,210,500,000,000 German marks. The wholesale PRICE index grew over 50 billion times during the same period. Every German citizen became a BILLIONAIRE, but most of them were of course hopelessly poor.

Notable & Quotable

"He was the president of the Reichsbank, whose principal obligation was supposed to be the preservation of the value of the CURRENCY, *proudly proclaiming to a group of parliamentarians that he now had the capacity to expand the* MONEY SUPPLY *by over 60 per cent in a single day and flood the country with even more paper."*
(Liaquat Ahamed: *Lords of Finance*, Windmill Books, 2010)

HOOVER, *Herbert*

Hoover took the oath of the presidential office in March 1929. A couple of months later, he saw WALL STREET tumble and the economy fall into a serious RECESSION. Although he tried to mend it, he missed the opportunity to fix the advancing BANKING CRISIS until it was too late; the GREAT DEPRESSION rolled out to its full strength, changing the USA and the rest of the world forever (and not for the better).

Devil's message: Learn ECONOMICS. *Then learn when to break the rules.*

KEYNES, *John Maynard*

Perhaps the most influential economist of the 20th century. Keynes proposed that GOVERNMENTS can borrow a lot of MONEY during the RECESSIONS and repay their DEBTS in the good times. This idea was perhaps not so bad in itself (some PEOPLE say), but has proven to be extremely prone to misinterpretation.

Keynes himself became most influential only after his DEATH in 1946, after which he could not protest against the misapplication of his theories by POLITICIANS the world over. POLITICIANS from different countries and different political backgrounds have usually used (and abused) only the first part of his advice: *"*GOVERNMENTS *can borrow a lot of* MONEY.*"* See KEYNESIANISM

Devil's message: Miraculous recipes for avoiding a RECESSION *can have serious side effects.*

LENIN, *Vladimir Ilyich*

No, Vladimir Ilyich. Killing off CAPITALISTS will not bring about instant PROSPERITY. Not even distant PROSPERITY.

Devil's message: Killing PEOPLE *doesn't generally bring about* ECONOMIC GROWTH.

LINDGRÉN, *Astrid*

The famous Swedish author of children's books. Her problem was too much success when Swedish income TAX RATES were at their peak. In 1976, Lindgrén's marginal tax rate rose to 102%. This led to political debate at the highest level. In the parliamentary ELECTIONS later the same year, the incumbent SOCIAL DEMOCRAT GOVERNMENT was voted out for the first time in 44 years. The Lindgrén TAX debate was one of several controversies that may have contributed to this result.

Devil's message: Write stories, become famous, change the world.

MARX, *Karl*

Surely a great man of incisive intellect; it's just a pity he based his life's work on the wrong assumption of the LABOUR THEORY OF VALUE, which, as we already know, can be proved false by the use of just three sandwiches (see SURPLUS VALUE). For this very simple reason all of his work has always been wrong.

Devil's message: Nothing is more powerful than a ridiculous mistake whose time has come.
See MARXISM, MARXIST ECONOMY, PROUDHON

MINSKY, *Hyman*

An insightful economist who elaborated the theory of the business cycle and CRISIS based upon BANK lending and the cycle of bad loans. BANKS lend more and more until the infamous MINSKY MOMENT arrives. Minsky, who lived from 1919 to 1996, saw the GREAT DEPRESSION unfold when he was merely a child. The theory he developed, however, would never be observed during his working life. No other major BANKING CRISIS in DEVELOPED MARKETS took place until 2007 and this is why Minsky was never truly vindicated or fully appreciated.

Minsky's name gained its fame (or notoriety) more than a decade after his DEATH—too late for him to enjoy his time in the spotlight.

Devil's message: Better to spot a great idea if you can enjoy its success during your own lifetime.

MITTERAND, *François*

Inviting communists into the GOVERNMENT in 1980 wasn't a particularly bright idea. FRANCE set out on the path towards ever-increasing UNEMPLOYMENT and GOVERNMENT DEBT RIGHT around that time. Also, nationalising a whole array of CORPORATIONS only to privatise them a couple of years later was a decidedly odd move.

Devil's message: Don't get your fingers burned putting them in the fire when countless others have already tried it before you.

NEHRU, *Jawaharlal*

Nehru was the architect of the Licence Raj system. This refers to the elaborate licences, regulations and accompanying red tape required to set up and run businesses in INDIA between 1947 and 1990. Licences were awarded only to a select few. Private CORPORATIONS were supervised and controlled by up to 80 GOVERNMENT agencies.

Reforms introduced after 1991 removed many of these restrictions, but Indian LABOUR laws still prevent manufacturers from reducing their workforce without prohibitive burdens. The LABOUR sector of the Indian economy consists of roughly 487 million workers. Of these, over 94 per cent work in unincorporated, 'unorganised enterprises'—firms which operate on the BLACK MARKET and ignore most laws and regulations. Their productivity is usually therefore very low, as are the wages. An unorganized enterprise has no access to CAPITAL and BANK CREDIT for further development; it cannot expand abroad and can't set up business partnerships with first-world CORPORATIONS.

Nehru's legacy costs INDIA incredible sums every year. See GANDHI

Devil's message: BUREAUCRACY *can be more destructive than war, colonialism, earthquakes, floods and epidemics combined.*

NOBEL, *Alfred*
Alfred Nobel was a highly successful entrepreneur. When a French journal erroneously published his obituary, Nobel realised that he would be remembered as an evil man who invented dynamite. He decided the very same day that he would build his immortality on establishing the eponymous endowment and prize.

However, he made one tiny mistake which could have undermined his legacy and rendered the NOBEL PRIZE irrelevant. He insisted that the NOBEL PRIZE Foundation PORTFOLIO be invested in safe SECURITIES. With the coming of INFLATION in the 20th century, managers of the endowment portfolio must have abandoned this stipulation and invested most of the MONEY under management in EQUITIES. Luckily for mankind, they saved it.

Devil's message: VALUE *preservation is not a* RISK *free business.*

PAHLAVI, *Mohammad Reza*

His 38-year rule in Iran ended in 1979. A benevolent monarch not without his achievements, but someone who didn't care all that much about the economy and was a tad too tolerant towards CORRUPTION. He also spent lavishly on luxuries and celebrations. The Islamic revolution that overthrew him shortly before his DEATH did not make the nation any happier.

Devil's message: The opulence of a ruler of a poor country raises a number of questions. Those questions can lead to answers, and the answers can have serious consequences.

POL POT
The leftist dictator of Cambodia during the 1970's. His extreme policies went as far as disbanding almost all authorities including the CENTRAL BANK, leaving only the army and the all-powerful police. He also banned CURRENCY and relocated the inhabitants of the capital city Phnom Penh out into the rice fields to work as peasants. After losing several million lives, the Cambodian nation was eventually happy to welcome the communist Vietnamese army as liberators.

Devil's message: Anti-establishment movements need to be subject to at least some constraints.

PROUDHON, *Pierre-Joseph*

You probably know CHURCHILL's famous quote about SOCIALISM meaning a fair share of misery, but perhaps you don't know who actually invented the idea of SOCIALISM and the fair share. Pierre-Joseph Proudhon (1809-1865) was a bankrupt printer who delved into philosophy to find the reason for his misfortune. He found it: private PROPERTY (which he lacked). Proudhon's principal conclusion was that 'PROPERTY is theft!' What is left, however, when a SOCIALIST GOVERNMENT bans PROPERTY? An equal share of misery, of course.

Ideas have consequences, and greatly mistaken ideas can have grave consequences. Karl MARX read Proudhon and instantly liked the idea of abolishing private PROPERTY. The two POVERTY-stricken intellectuals became great friends. Their friendship ended, however, when MARX responded to Proudhon's tract 'The Philosophy of POVERTY' with the provocatively entitled 'The POVERTY of Philosophy'. Few PEOPLE have paid attention to Proudhon ever since as MARX proved to be a much more captivating writer (and MARX's full beard proved to be more picturesque than Proudhon's).

Devil's message: Behind every bitter intellectual BANKRUPTCY there is an embittered bankrupt intellectual.

ROOSEVELT, *Franklin Delano*

The architect of the NEW DEAL. Some of his tricks weren't all that bad. Hiking income TAX up to 79 per cent during peacetime was not such a great idea, however, as it prolonged the GREAT DEPRESSION. Retail PRICE regulation was equally unsuccessful in thwarting DEFLATION.

Devil's message: Want to snuff out economic recovery right from the start? Raise taxes. Simple!

Notable & Quotable
"In their understanding of the Depression, ROOSEVELT and his economic advisers had cause and effect reversed. They did not recognize that PRICES had fallen because of the Depression. They believed that the Depression prevailed because PRICES had fallen. The obvious remedy, then, was to raise PRICES, which they decided to do by creating artificial shortages. Hence arose a collection of crackpot policies designed to cure the Depression

by cutting back on production. The scheme was so patently self-defeating that it's hard to believe anyone seriously believed it would work."
(Robert Higgs: *How FDR Made the Depression Worse*, The MISES Institute Monthly, February 1995)

SCHACHT, *Hjalmar Horace Greeley*

Schacht was revered as the finance minister who ended von Havenstein's HYPERINFLATION in 1923 and reintroduced the gold-backed Reichsmark in remarkably quick time. When Hitler came to POWER, Schacht was appointed as Minister for the Economy, or Wirtschaftsminister. (The German Ministry of Finance was a different and less powerful institution. Its most important task at the time was the confiscation of Jewish PROPERTY.)

Schacht engineered GERMANY's economic recovery in the 1930's, but also found ingenious ways of financing the preparations for WWII. A great economist who sold his soul to serve evil.

Schacht was later dismissed from all his public functions in Hitler's GERMANY. In 1943, he was even arrested and sent to a concentration camp. The Nuremberg trials acquitted Schacht, but no one could deny his contribution to Hitler's rise to POWER.

Devil's message: The more valuable your skills, the greater the sin in donating them to an evil cause.

STALIN, *Iossif Vissarionovich*

The Soviet leader whose nom de guerre was derived from the word "steel", later to become synonymous with the heavy-handed, command-and-control style of economic governance. Being typical of the real SOCIALIST countries up until the late 1980's, this was the main reason the soviets lost the Cold WAR. See COMPETITION

Devil's message: You cannot command-and-control the economy. It will not obey. Not even at gunpoint.

THATCHER, *Margaret*

Thatcher has been dividing British public opinion ever since she entered Downing Street in 1979. The indisputable fact is that she left the British economy in better shape in 1990 than it had been when she found it. By all reasonable measures, Britain was better off after Thatcher than before her.

Yet she, too, made mistakes. The poll TAX, for instance. PEOPLE hate TAXES that do not reflect differences in PROPERTY and income. The poll tax was considered unjust even by many Thatcherites and this brought about the Iron Lady's resignation.

Devil's message: TAXES *are a tricky thing.*

DE VALÉRA, *Éamon*

Saw Ireland as the land of saints and scholars, poets and fairies, myths and legends. He did not think the economy was important; it was. As a result of de Valéra's policies, Ireland remained poor and underdeveloped for a very long time.

Devil's message: Again and again, it's the economy, stupid.

WILSON, *Harold*

During his two terms as Prime Minister, Wilson presided over significant increases in the overall TAX burden in the UK. In 1965, he introduced the Capital Gains TAX. In the 1970's, his GOVERNMENT set up an income TAX system which included a 98 per cent marginal rate of personal income TAX for top earners. Shortly after he resigned in 1976, Britain needed to ask the IMF for assistance. Wilson was made immortal by The Beatles in the lyrics of *Taxman*, a song from the 1966 album *Revolver*:

Let me tell you how it will be
There's one for you, nineteen for me
'Cause I'm the taxman, yeah, I'm the taxman

Should five per cent appear too small
Be thankful I don't take it all
'Cause I'm the taxman, yeah, I'm the taxman

If you drive a car, I'll tax the street,
If you try to sit, I'll tax your seat.
If you get too cold, I'll tax the heat,
If you take a walk, I'll tax your feet.

Don't ask me what I want it for
If you don't want to pay some more
'Cause I'm the taxman, yeah, I'm the taxman

Now my advice for those who die
Declare the pennies on your eyes
'Cause I'm the taxman, yeah, I'm the taxman
And you're working for no one but me.

(George Harrison)

And the winner of the Devil's Prize for the Most Epic Economic and Financial Failure is...

MAO ZEDONG

As leader of the PEOPLE's Republic of CHINA, he conceived the campaign called "The Great Leap Forward" from 1958 to 1961. Private farming was prohibited and those engaged in it were persecuted and labelled as counter-revolutionaries. The Great Leap ended in catastrophe. Estimates of the DEATH toll range from 18 million to 45 million PEOPLE.

As if this were not bad enough, the Cultural REVOLUTION was launched in 1966. Millions of PEOPLE were persecuted and suffered a wide range of abuses including public humiliation, arbitrary imprisonment, torture, sustained harassment, the seizure of PROPERTY, and forcible transfers of urban youth to rural regions. CHINA deliberately destroyed its historic relics, artefacts and buildings. Out of a total of 6000 Tibetan monasteries, only a dozen were left undamaged. The scope of destruction was without precedent. A civilisation which had endured for millennia disappeared within two or three very short years.

The Chinese economy was devastated. When the future Chinese premier Deng Xiaoping led a delegation to the United Nations in New York in 1974, Chinese officials discovered, as they prepared for the somewhat expensive trip, that they could muster only $38,000 in foreign cash between them. In those days there were no BANKS in CHINA except the PEOPLE's BANK of CHINA, then a department of the Ministry of Finance.

To this day, however, CHINA exhibits Mao Zedong's portrait on its banknotes. As a disclaimer for INVESTORS, perhaps.

DEVIL'S MESSAGE:
YOU CAN DESTROY
THOUSANDS OF YEARS OF CIVILISATION
IN THE BLINK OF AN EYE.
YES, YOU CAN.

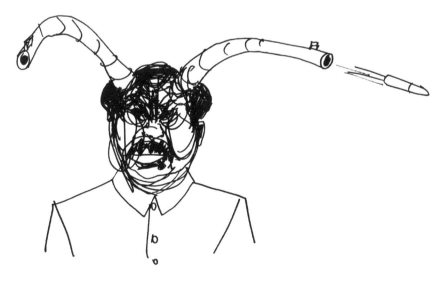

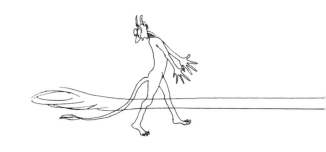

investing in antiques

czech-antiques.com

the internet catalogue of antique galleries

VÝROBA PONOŽEK

www.otocr.cz

The Devil's Fashion Collection

LUXURY SOCKS
with woven portrait of Murray Rothbard
or Ludwig von Mises
Best quality cotton, gift wrapped

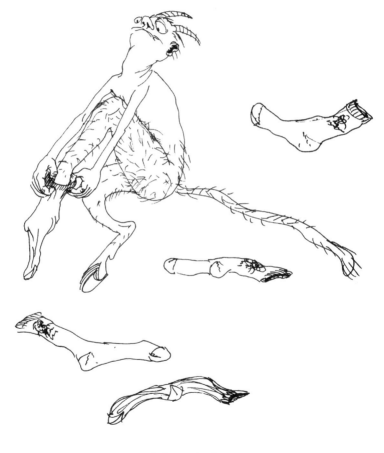

www.internetart.cz
info@internetart.cz

In the gallery you can find the works of Klára Pernicová, the illustrator of this book.
Klára Pernicová (1985) studied arts in Prague and Helsinki, graduated as Master of Arts from the Academy of Fine Arts in Prague (School of Intemedia Studies of Professor Milan Knížák). Klára is an illustrator, designer, sculptor and medial artist.

investing in art

czech-art.com

Luxurious handmade silk ties & scarves.
Limited collections of exclusive handicrafts.
www.lee-oppenheimer.com

The Devil is in Detail

. Angel investments

. High income investing

. Peer to Peer lending

. Tailored wealth management solutions

At Symfonie Capital our mission is to provide investors not just investments, but also the tools, expertise and personal dedication it takes to make investments that generate returns. We've assembled a team of internationally experienced finance professionals and successful entrepreneurs who add value at each stage of the investment process - starting with pre-deal research and ending with the day we finally exit.

Symfonie

www.symfoniecapital.com
info@symfoniecapital.com

DEVIL'S NOTES:

DEVIL'S NOTES:

DEVIL'S NOTES:

DEVIL'S NOTES:

DEVIL'S NOTES:

DEVIL'S NOTES:

DEVIL'S NOTES:

DEVIL'S NOTES:

DEVIL'S NOTES:

DEVIL'S NOTES:

www.hyde-park-publishing.co.uk
www.devilsdictionaries.com
Twitter: @DevilinFinance